David Gray White Ladder

**(precedes track 1: backtrack to -2.01)

Music arranged by Matt Cowe
Music engraved by Andrew Shiels

Printed in the United Kingdom by
Caligraving Limited, Thetford, Norfolk.

Guitar Tablature Explained

Guitar music can be notated three different ways: on a musical stave, in tablature, and in rhythm slashes

RHYTHM SLASHES are written above the stave. Strum chords in the rhythm indicated. Round noteheads indicate single notes.

THE MUSICAL STAVE shows pitches and rhythms and is divided by lines into bars. Pitches are named after the first seven letters of the alphabet.

TABLATURE graphically represents the guitar fingerboard. Each horizontal line represents a string, and each number represents a fret.

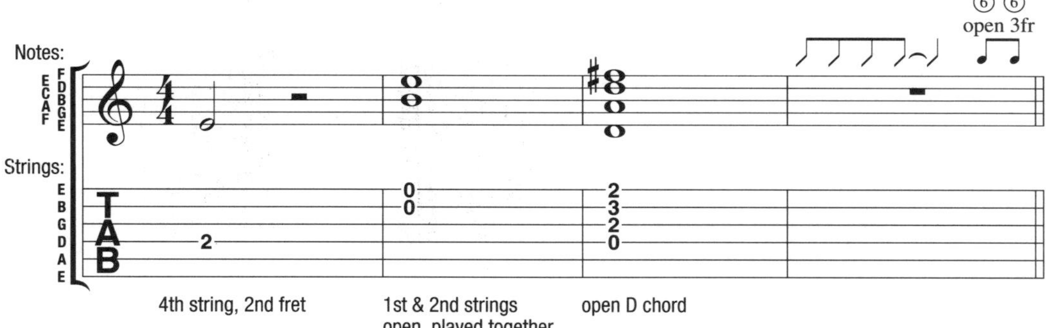

definitions for special guitar notation

SEMI-TONE BEND: Strike the note and bend up a semi-tone (1/2 step).

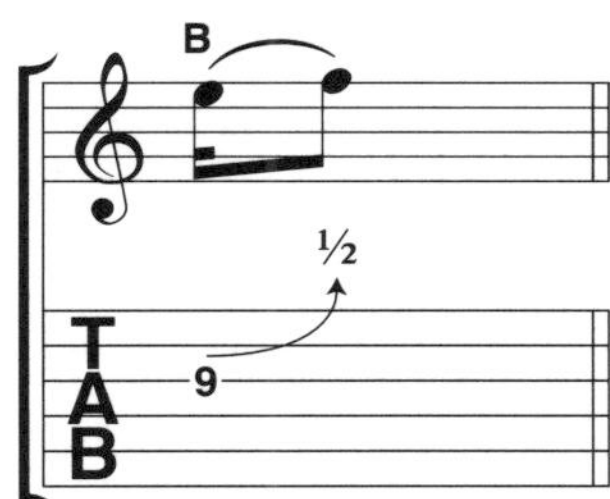

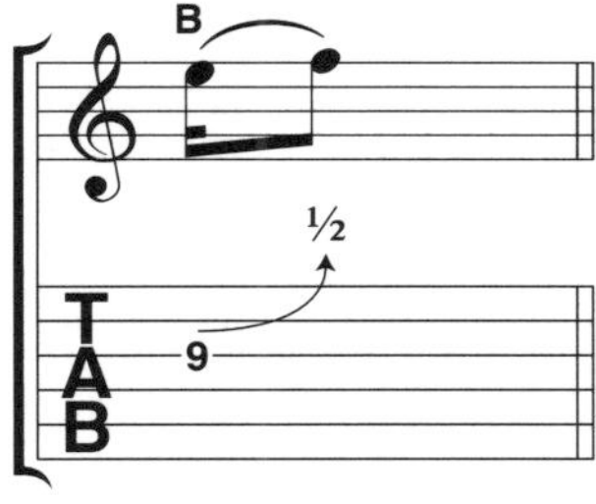

WHOLE-TONE BEND: Strike the note and bend up a whole-tone (whole step).

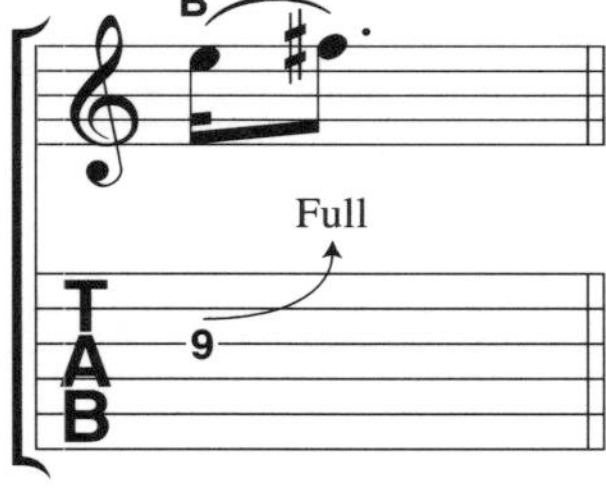

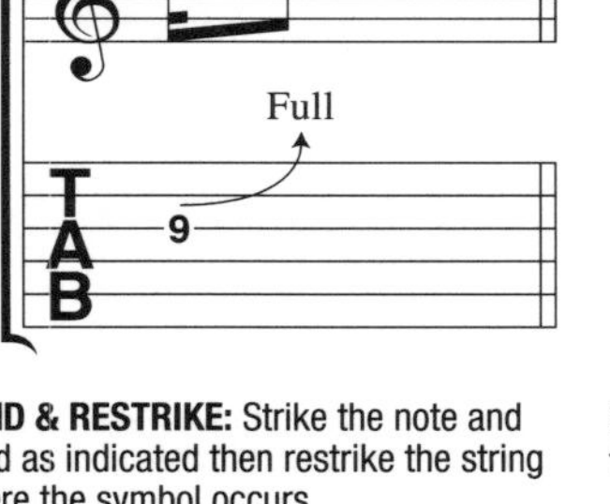

GRACE NOTE BEND: Strike the note and bend as indicated. Play the first note as quickly as possible.

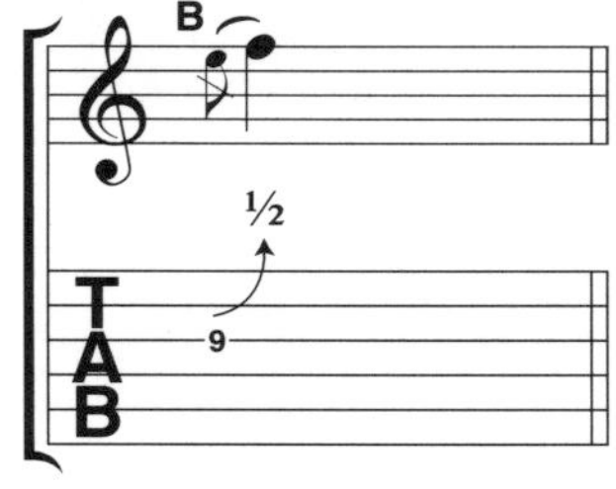

QUARTER-TONE BEND: Strike the note and bend up a 1/4 step.

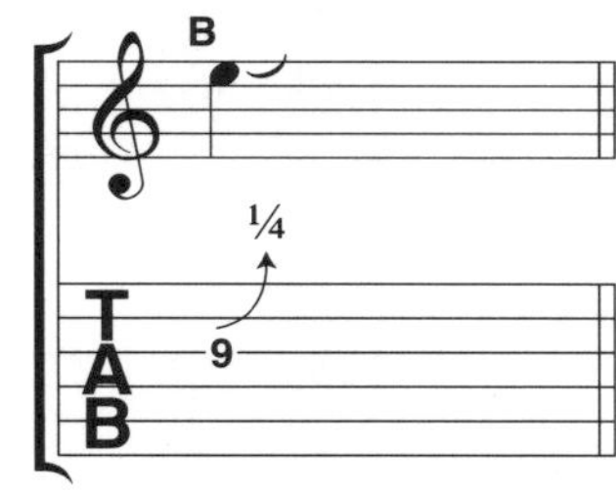

BEND & RELEASE: Strike the note and bend up as indicated, then release back to the original note.

BEND & RESTRIKE: Strike the note and bend as indicated then restrike the string where the symbol occurs.

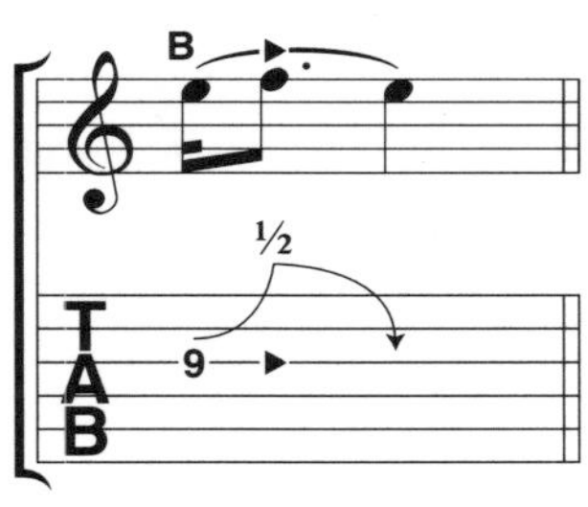

PRE-BEND: Bend the note as indicated, then strike it.

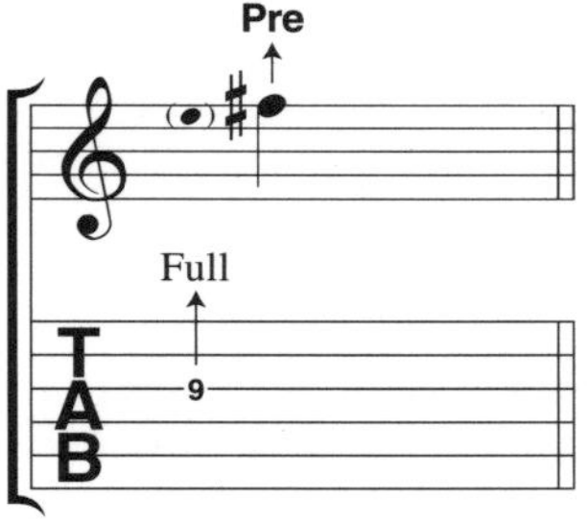

PRE-BEND & RELEASE: Bend the note as indicated. Strike it and release the note back to the original pitch.

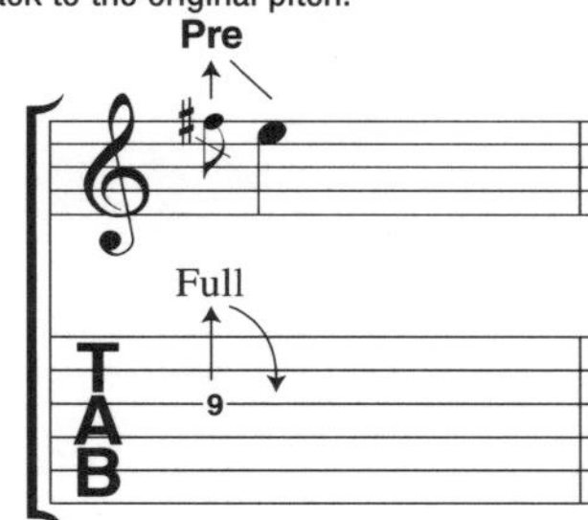

HAMMER-ON: Strike the first (lower) note with one finger, then sound the higher note (on the same string) with another finger by fretting it without picking.

PULL-OFF: Place both fingers on the notes to be sounded. Strike the first note and without picking, pull the finger off to sound the second (lower) note.

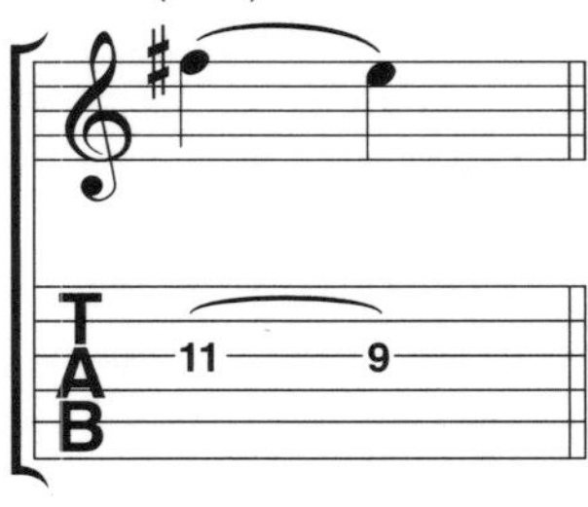

LEGATO SLIDE (GLISS): Strike the first note and then slide the same fret-hand finger up or down to the second note. The second note is not struck.

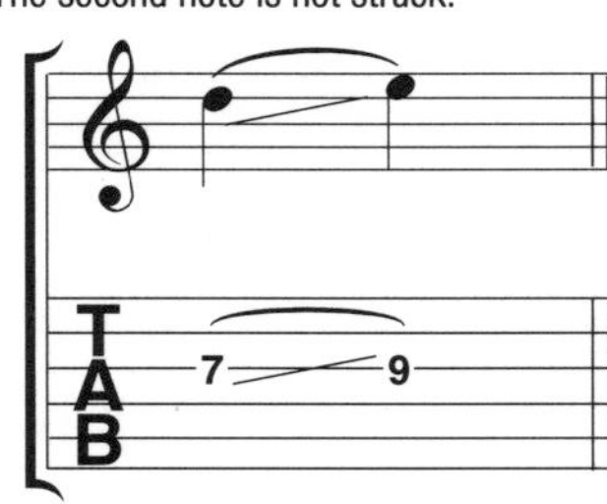

SHIFT SLIDE (GLISS & RESTRIKE): Same as legato slide, except the second note is struck.

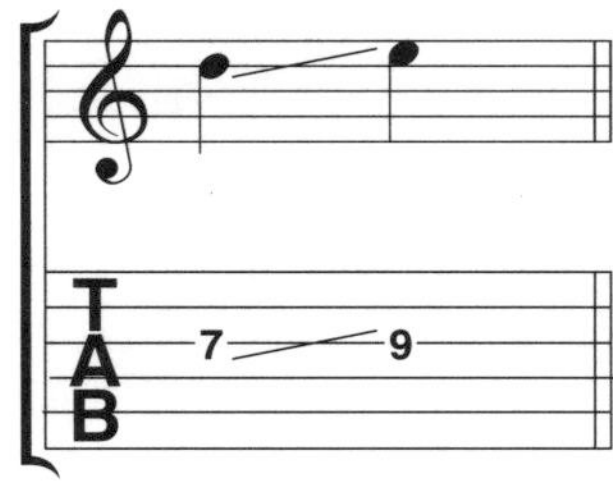

NATURAL HARMONIC: Strike the note while the fret-hand lightly touches the string directly over the fret indicated.

PICK SCRAPE: The edge of the pick is rubbed down (or up) the string, producing a scratchy sound.

PALM MUTING: The note is partially muted by the pick hand lightly touching the string(s) just before the bridge.

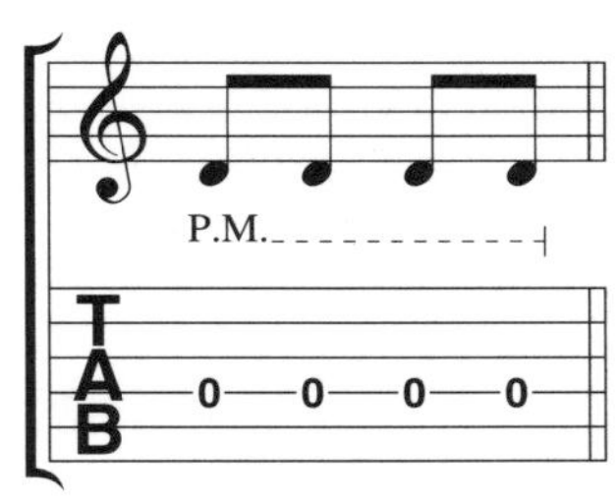

MUFFLED STRINGS: A percussive sound is produced by laying the fret hand across the string(s) without depressing, and striking them with the pick hand.

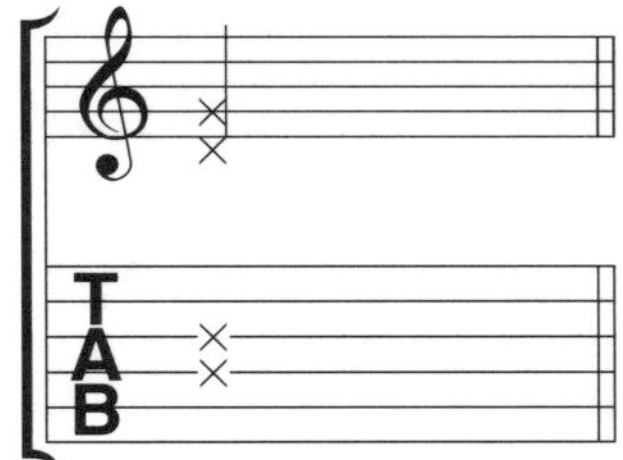

NOTE: The speed of any bend is indicated by the music notation and tempo.

Babylon

Words & Music by David Gray

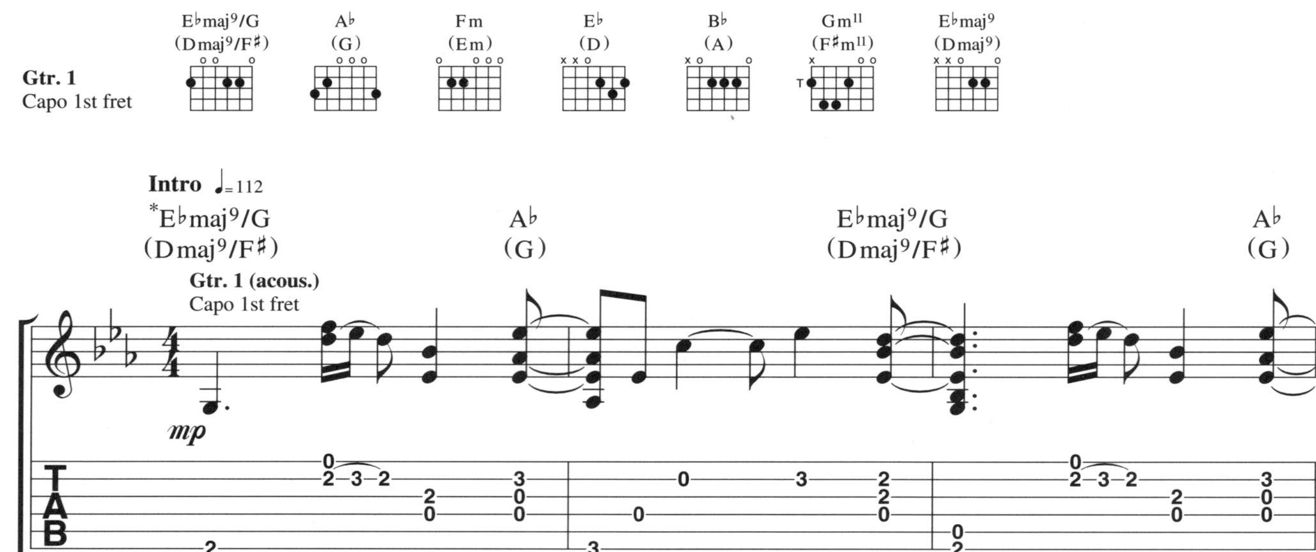

* Symbols in parentheses represent chord names with respect to capoed gtr. (Tab 0 = 1st fret)
Symbols above represent actual sounding chords.

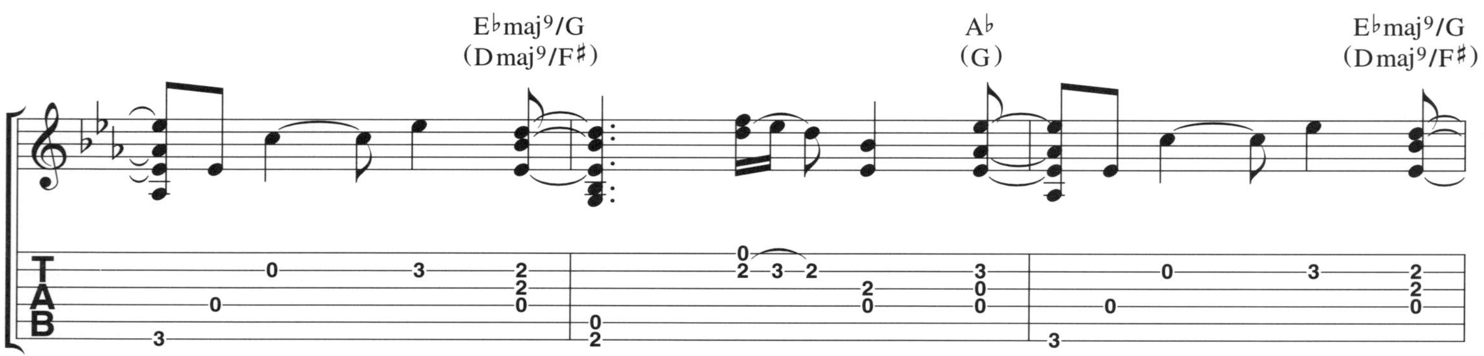

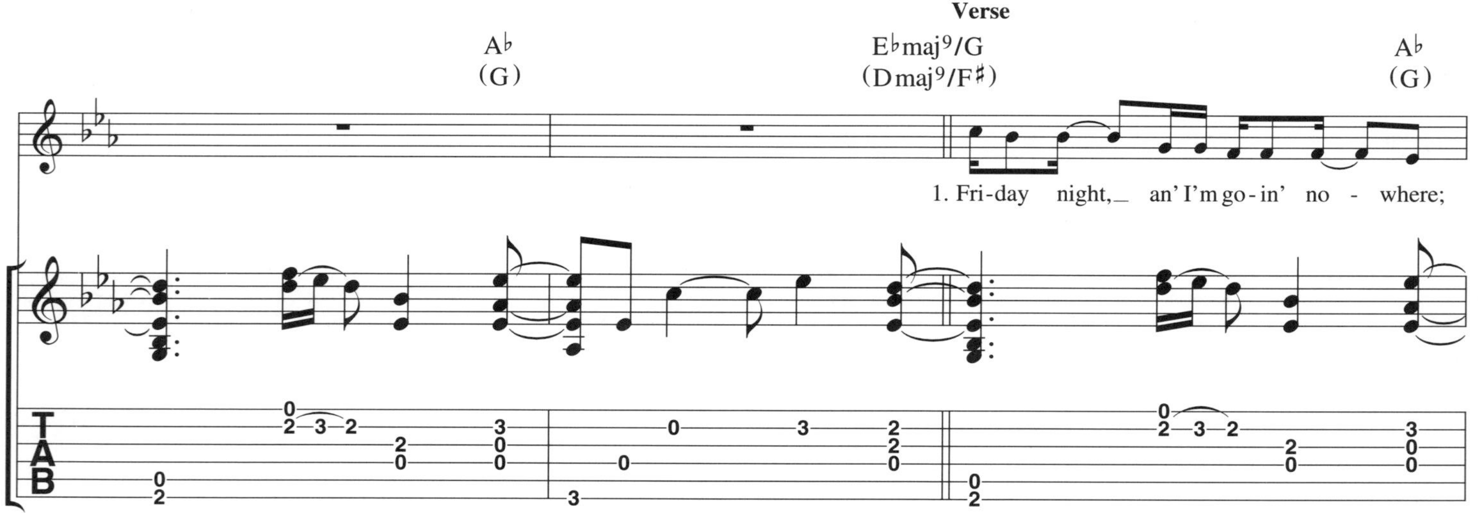

E♭maj9/G
(Dmaj9/F♯)
A♭
(G)
E♭maj9/G
(Dmaj9/F♯)
all the lights are chang - in' green to red.
Turn-in' ov - er T. V. sta - tions, si - tu - a - tions run-nin' through my
head.
Look-in' back through time, you know it's clear
that I've been blind I've been a fool.
To op -

A♭
(G)
E♭maj9/G
(Dmaj9/F♯)
en up my heart to all that jea-lous-y that bit-ter-ness, that
Fm
(Em)
ri-di-cule.
Verse
2. Sat-ur-day I'm run-nin' wild, an' all the lights are chang-in' red
3. Sun-day all the lights in Lon-don shin-ing, sky is fad-ing red
to green.
to blue.

A♭ (G)
E♭maj9/G (Dmaj9/F♯)
Mov-in' through_ the crowds,_ I'm push-in' chem-i-cals__ are rush-in' in__ my__
Kick-ing through_ the au-tumn leaves an' won-derin' where it is you might_ be__
__ blood-stream. On-ly wish_
__ go-ing to.
__ that you__ were here,__ you know_ I'm seein'__ it so__ clear;__ I've__ been a-
Turn-in' back__ for home__ you know_ I'm feel-ing so a-lone__ I___ can't be-
-fraid___ to show_
-lieve.___
T
A
B

A♭
(G)
E♭maj9/G
(Dmaj9/F♯)
you how I real - ly feel, ad - mit to some of those bad mis -
Climb - in' on the stair I turn a - round to see you smil-ing there in
takes I've made.
front of me.
Pre-chorus
E♭
(D)
B♭
(A)
An' if you want it come an' get it,
Fm
(Em)
Gm11
(F♯m11)
for cry - in' out loud.
The love that I was
optional Thumb plays 6th string
(T)

B♭
(A)
Fm
(Em)
A♭
(G)
giv-in' you was never in doubt.
Chorus
E♭
(D)
B♭
(A)
Fm
(Em)
mf
Let go your heart, let go your head and feel it now.
Let go your heart, let go your head, and feel it now,
1.
To Coda
Ba - by - lon,

1. cont.
E♭maj9/G
(Dmaj9/F♯)
A♭
(G)
Ba - by - lon,
mp
D.S. al Coda
2.
B♭
(A)
now.
Coda
now,
Ba - by - lon,

E♭maj9/G
(Dmaj9/F♯)
A♭
(G)
E♭maj9/G
(Dmaj9/F♯)
Ba - by - lon,
Ba - by - lon,
A♭
(G)
E♭maj9/G
(Dmaj9/F♯)
A♭
(G)
Ba - by - lon,
E♭maj9/G
(Dmaj9/F♯)
A♭
(G)
E♭maj9/G
(Dmaj9/F♯)
Ba - by - lon,
ah.
E♭maj9
(Dmaj9)
TAB

Please forgive me

Words & Music by David Gray

Am11
G13
Cadd9
Em7
Feels like light - ning run-ning through
Want to tell you just how good
Am11
G13
F
my veins
it feels,
ev - 'ry time I look
when you look at me that way,
C
Gsus4
To Coda 1
F
To Coda 3
To Coda 2
at you,
ah,
ev - 'ry time I look at
when you look at me that
Cadd9
Em7
Am11
G13
you.
way.
TAB

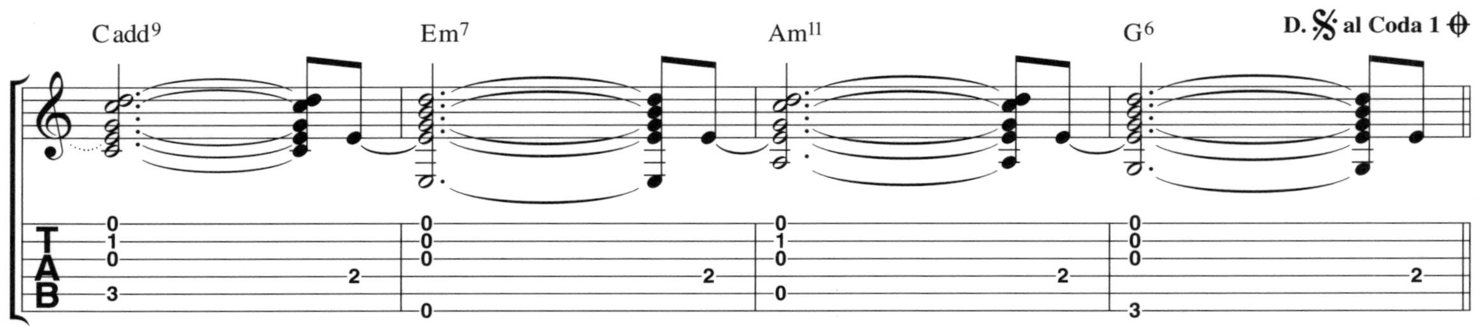
Cadd9
Em7
Am11
G6
D.𝄋 al Coda 1 𝄌

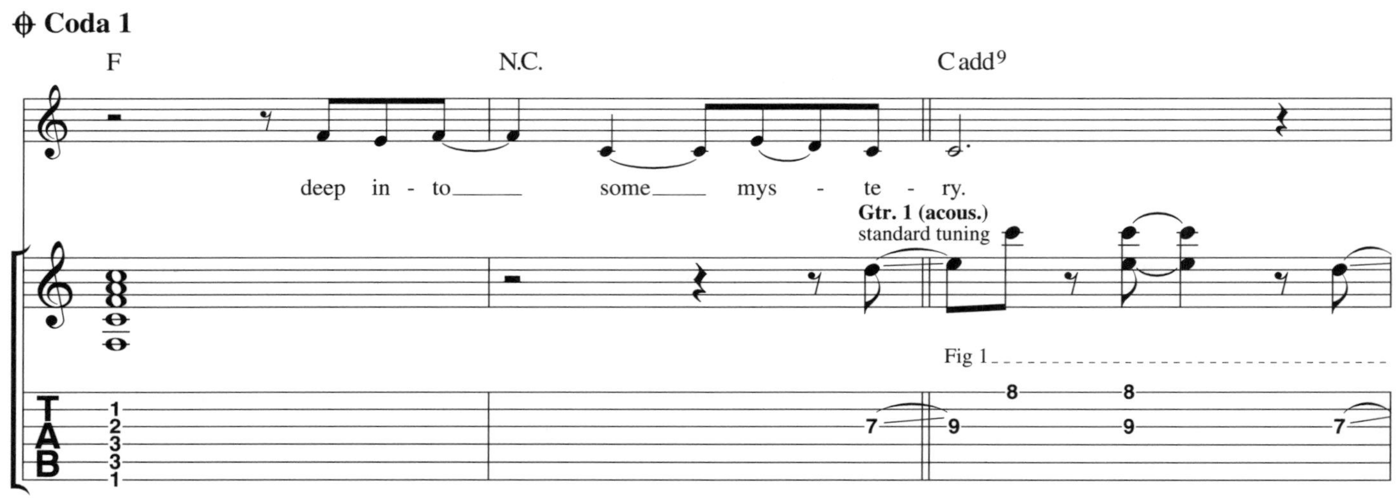
𝄌 Coda 1
F
N.C.
Cadd9
deep in - to some mys - te - ry.
Gtr. 1 (acous.)
standard tuning
Fig 1

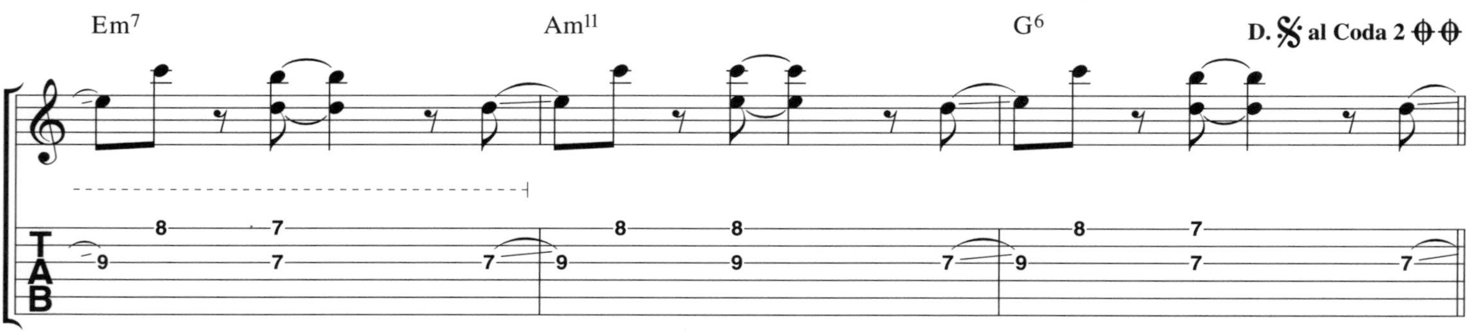
Em7
Am11
G6
D.𝄋 al Coda 2 𝄌𝄌

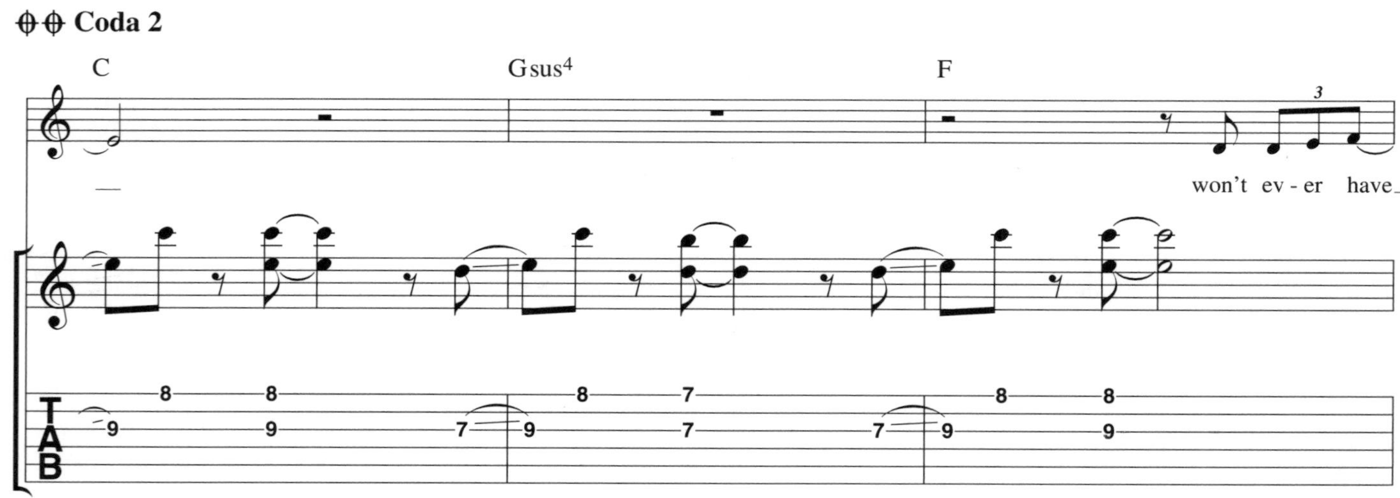
𝄌𝄌 Coda 2
C
Gsus4
F
won't ev - er have

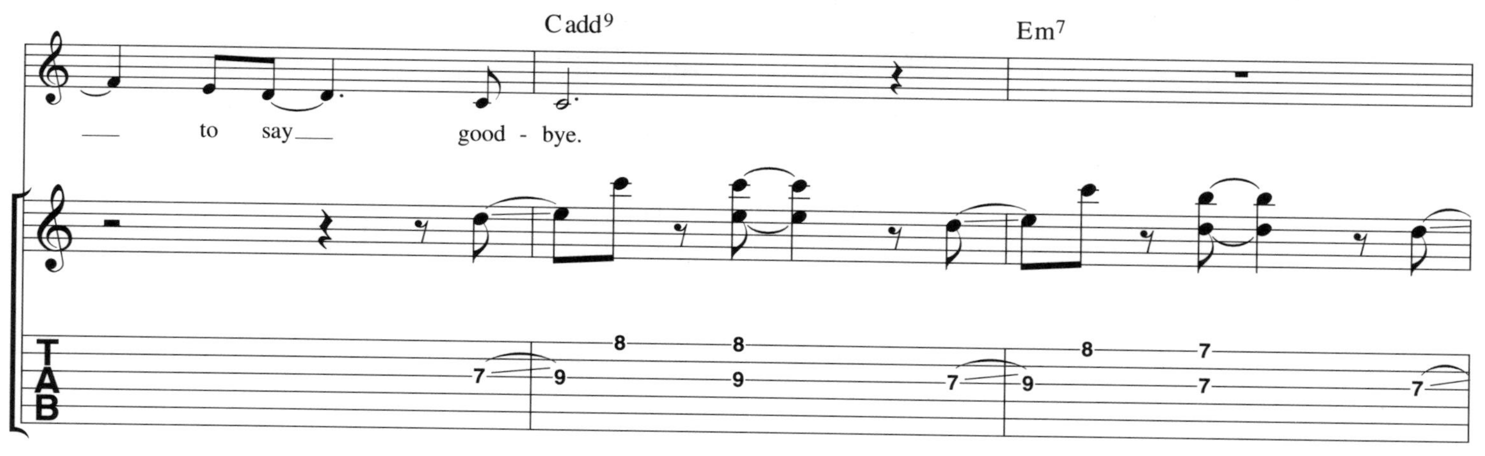
Cadd9
Em7
— to say— good - bye.
T
A
B

Am11
G13
Cadd9
Em7
Woh,— woh,— I
T
A
B

Am11
G13
F
woh,— woh,— I.
T
A
B

C
Gsus4
F
D.𝄋 al Coda 3
T
A
B

Coda 3

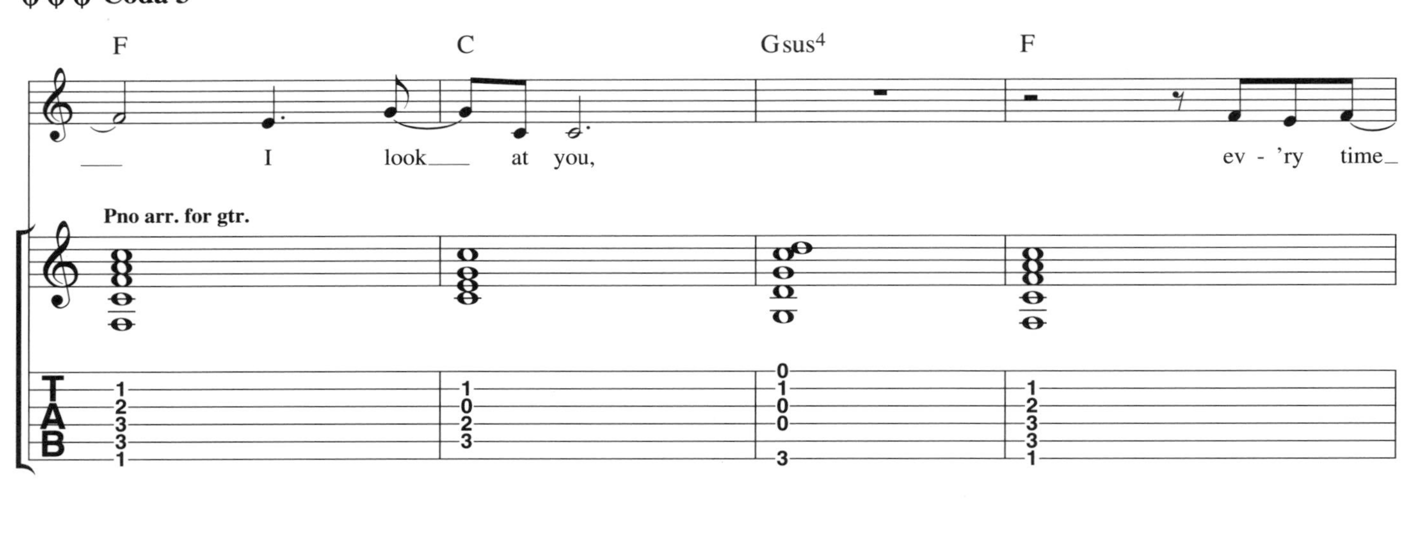
F
C
Gsus4
F
I look at you,
ev - 'ry time
Pno arr. for gtr.

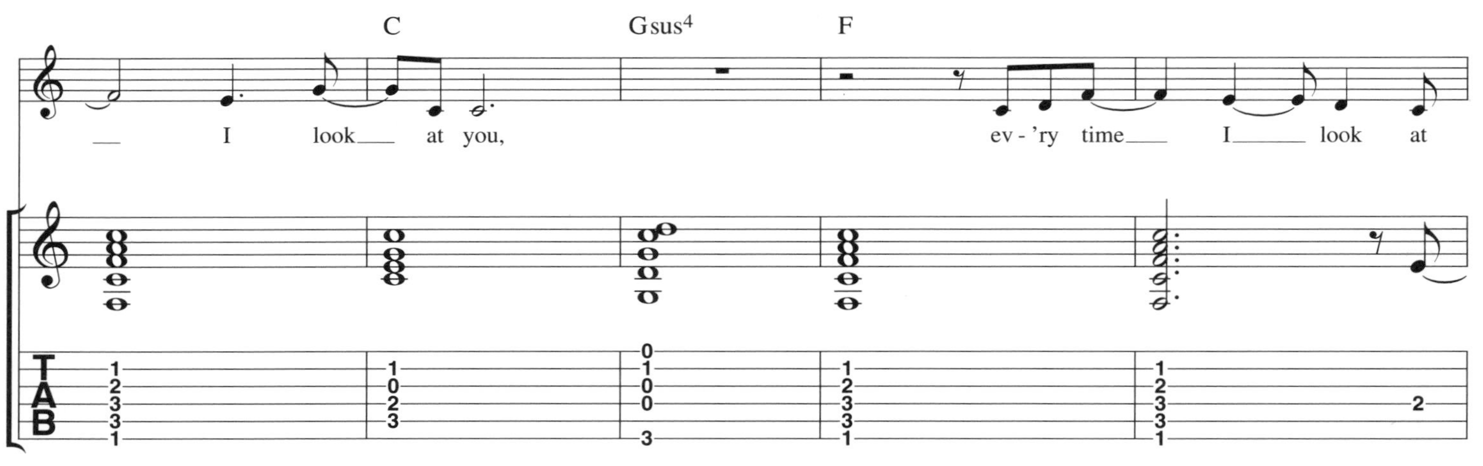
C
Gsus4
F
I look at you,
ev - 'ry time I look at

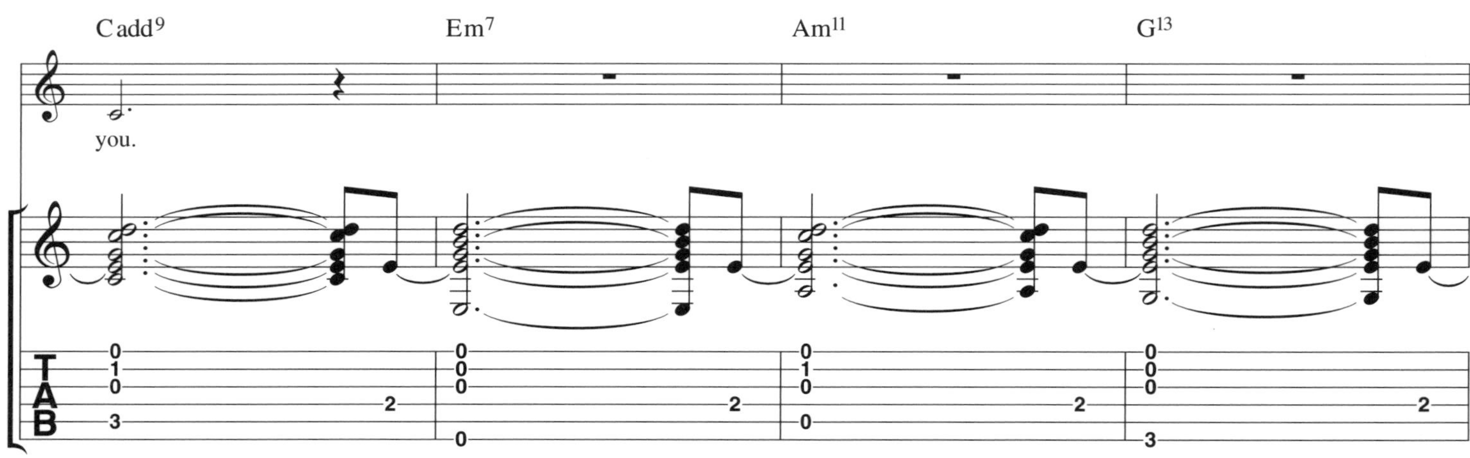
Cadd9
Em7
Am11
G13
you.

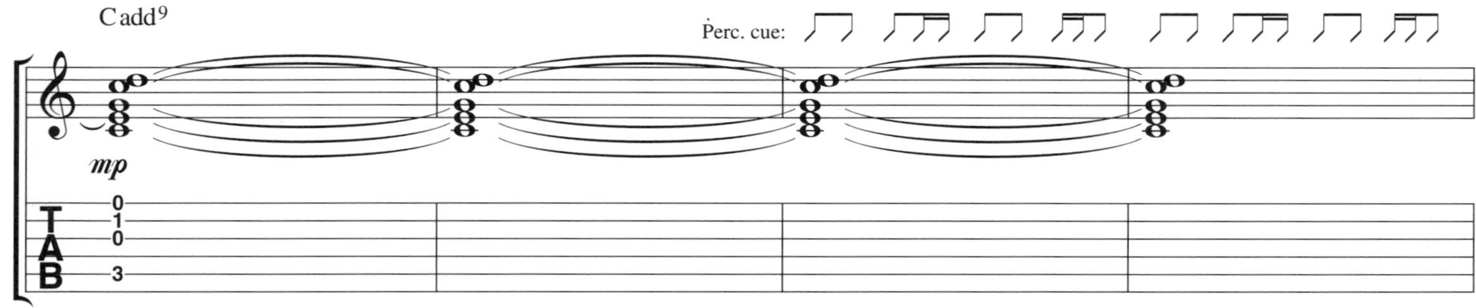
Cadd9
Perc. cue:
mp

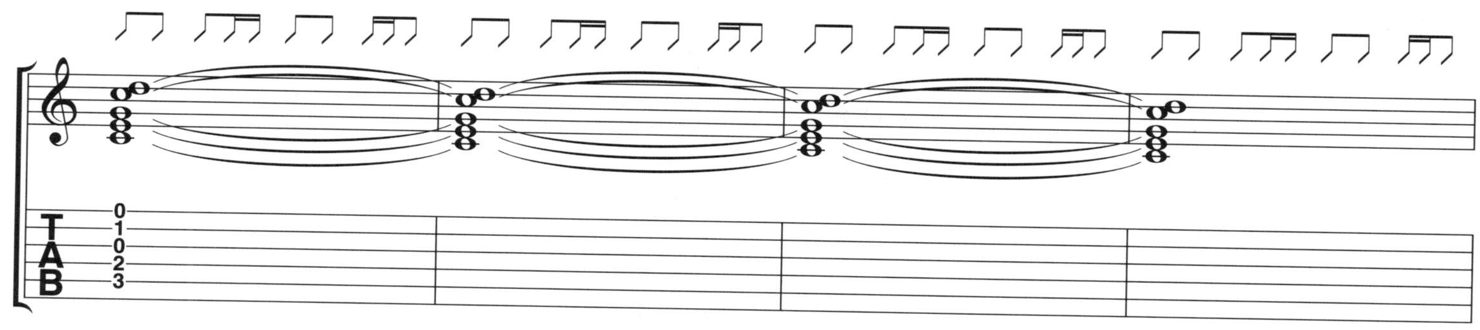

Cadd9
1.
2.
Gtr. 1
Bass cue:

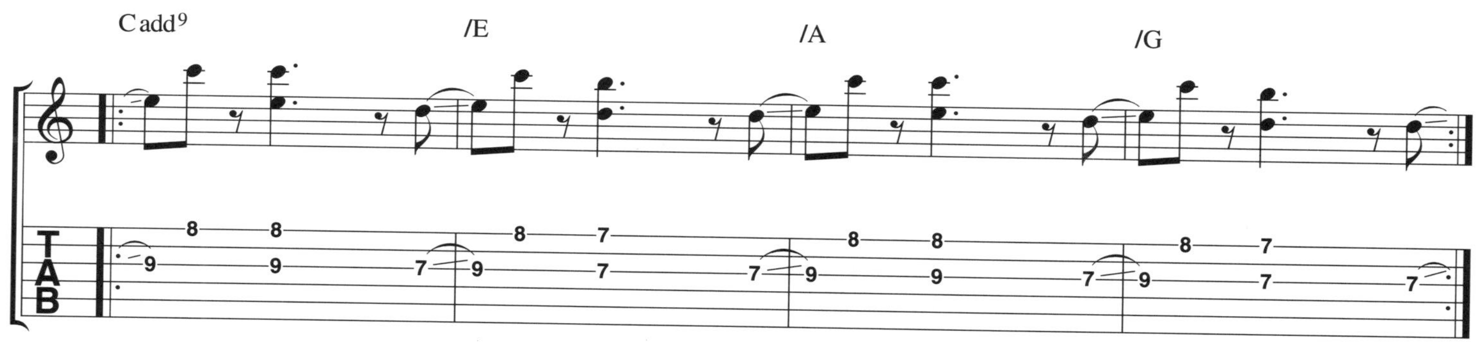
Cadd9
/E
/A
/G

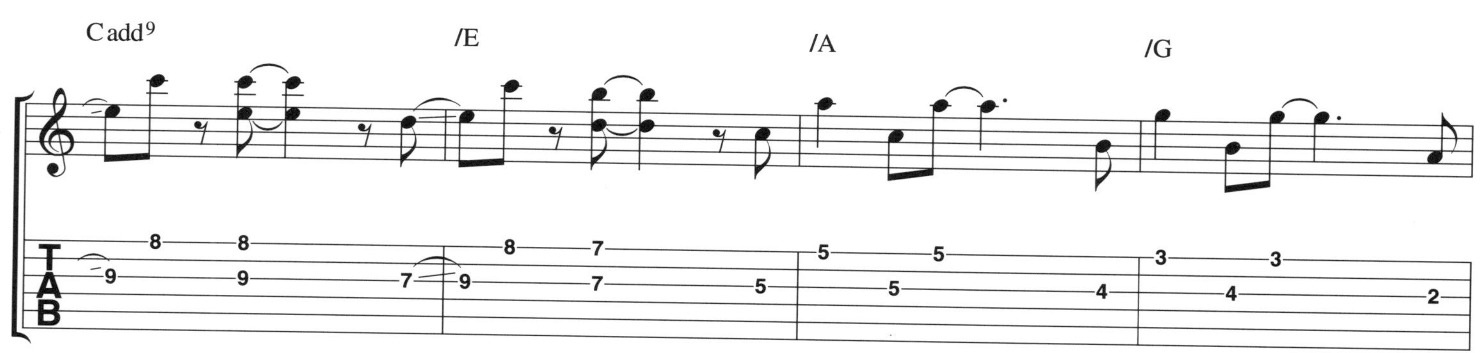
Cadd9
/E
/A
/G

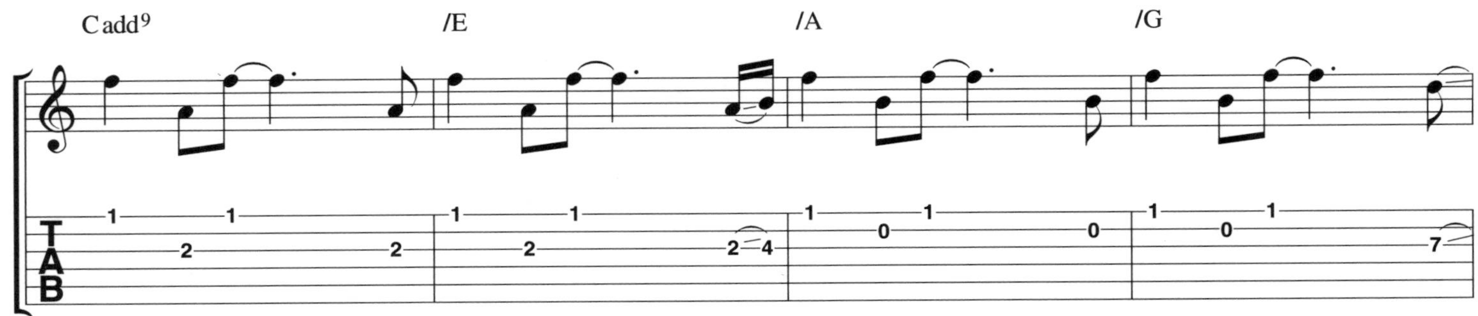

Verse 3:

Throw a stone and watch the ripples flow
Moving out across the bay
Like a stone, I fall into your eyes
Deep into that mystery
Ah, deep into some mystery.

Verse 4:

I got half a mind to scream out loud
I got half a mind to die
So I won't ever have to lose you, girl
Won't ever have to say goodbye, bye, bye
I won't ever have to lie
Won't ever have to say goodbye.

My oh my

Words & Music by David Gray & Craig McClune

All gtrs tuned
⑥ = D ③ = G
⑤ = A ② = A
④ = D ① = D
Capo 5th fret

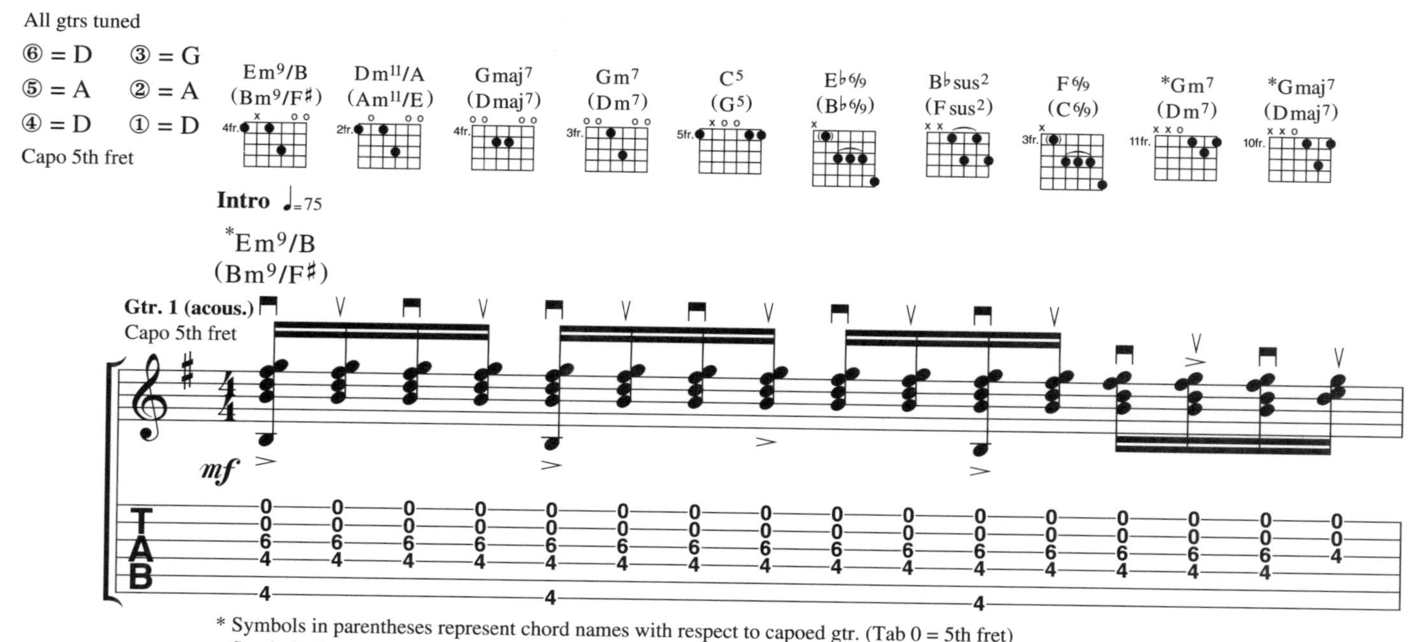

* Symbols in parentheses represent chord names with respect to capoed gtr. (Tab 0 = 5th fret)
Symbols above represent actual sounding chords.

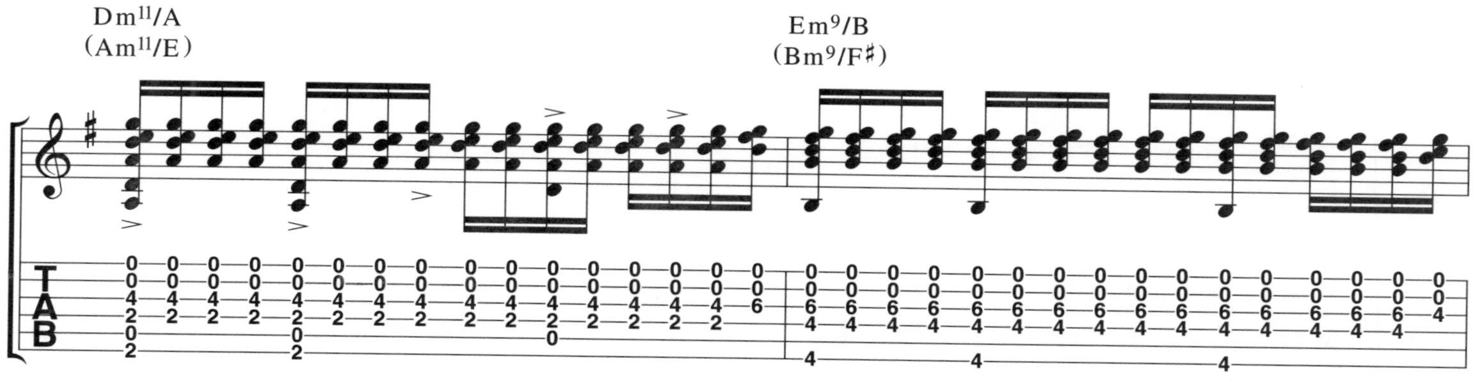

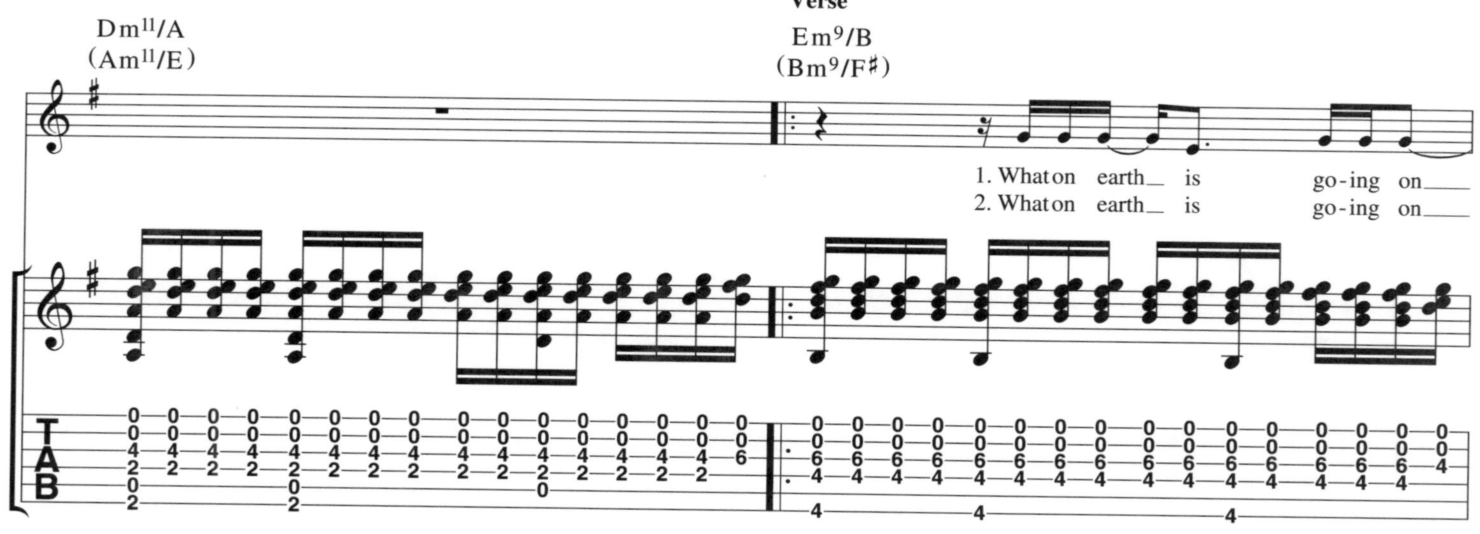

Dm11/A
(Am11/E)
Em9/B
(Bm9/F♯)
in my heart? Has it turned as cold as stone?
in my head? You know I used to be so sure.
Dm11/A
(Am11/E)
Em9/B
(Bm9/F♯)
Seems these days I don't feel
You know I used to be so de-fin-
Dm11/A
(Am11/E)
Em9/B
(Bm9/F♯)
an-y-thing 'less it cuts me right down to the bone.
-ite, thought I knew what love was for.
Dm11/A
(Am11/E)
Em9/B
(Bm9/F♯)
What on earth is go-ing on
I look a-round these days,
Fig. 1

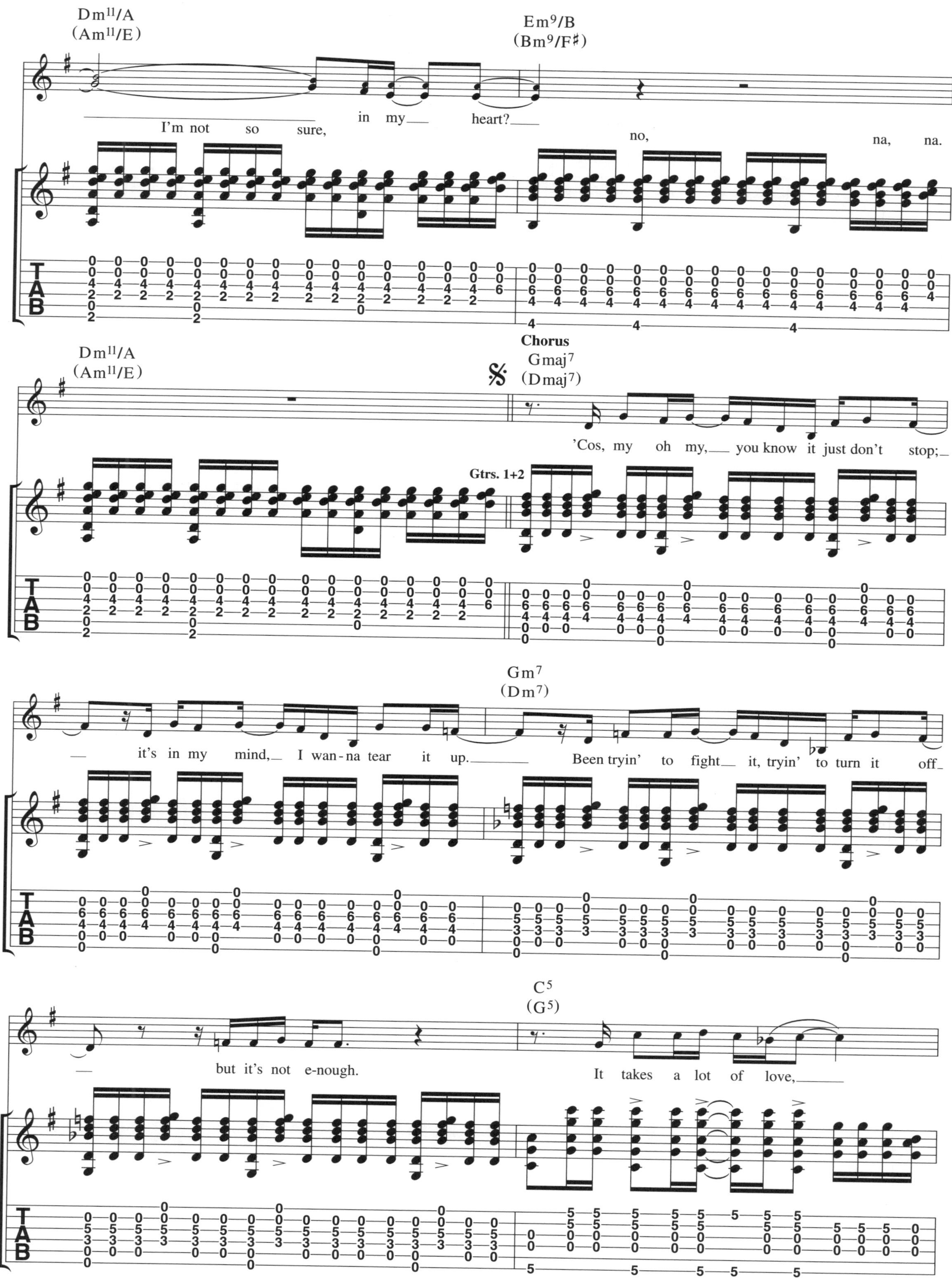

Dm11/A
(Am11/E)
Em9/B
(Bm9/F♯)
I'm not so sure, in my heart?
no, na, na.
Chorus
Gmaj7
(Dmaj7)
'Cos, my oh my, you know it just don't stop;
Gtrs. 1+2
it's in my mind, I wan-na tear it up.
Gm7
(Dm7)
Been tryin' to fight it, tryin' to turn it off
but it's not e-nough.
C5
(G5)
It takes a lot of love,

E♭6/9
(B♭6/9)
B♭sus2
(F sus2)
it takes a lot of love, my friend to keep your heart from freez - ing
* optional
E♭6/9
(B♭6/9)
F6/9
(C6/9)
To Coda
1.
Gmaj7
(Dmaj7)
to push on till the end.
My oh my.
1. cont.
2.
Gmaj7
(Dmaj7)
And, my oh my you know I just can't win;
Gm7
(Dm7)
I burn it down, it comes right back a - gain. What kind of world is this we're liv - ing in,

C5
(G5)
where you nev - er win?
It takes a lot - ta love,
E♭6/9
(B♭6/9)
B♭sus2
(F sus2)
it takes a lot - ta love these days
to keep your heart from freez - ing,
E♭6/9
(B♭6/9)
F 6/9
(C 6/9)
Em9/B
(Bm9/F♯)
to keep your spi - rit free.
A
Gtr. 2
mp
Gtr. 1 cont sim.
Dm11/A
(Am11/E)
Em9/B
(Bm9/F♯)
Dm11/A
(Am11/E)
D.S. al Coda
ha.
My oh my.

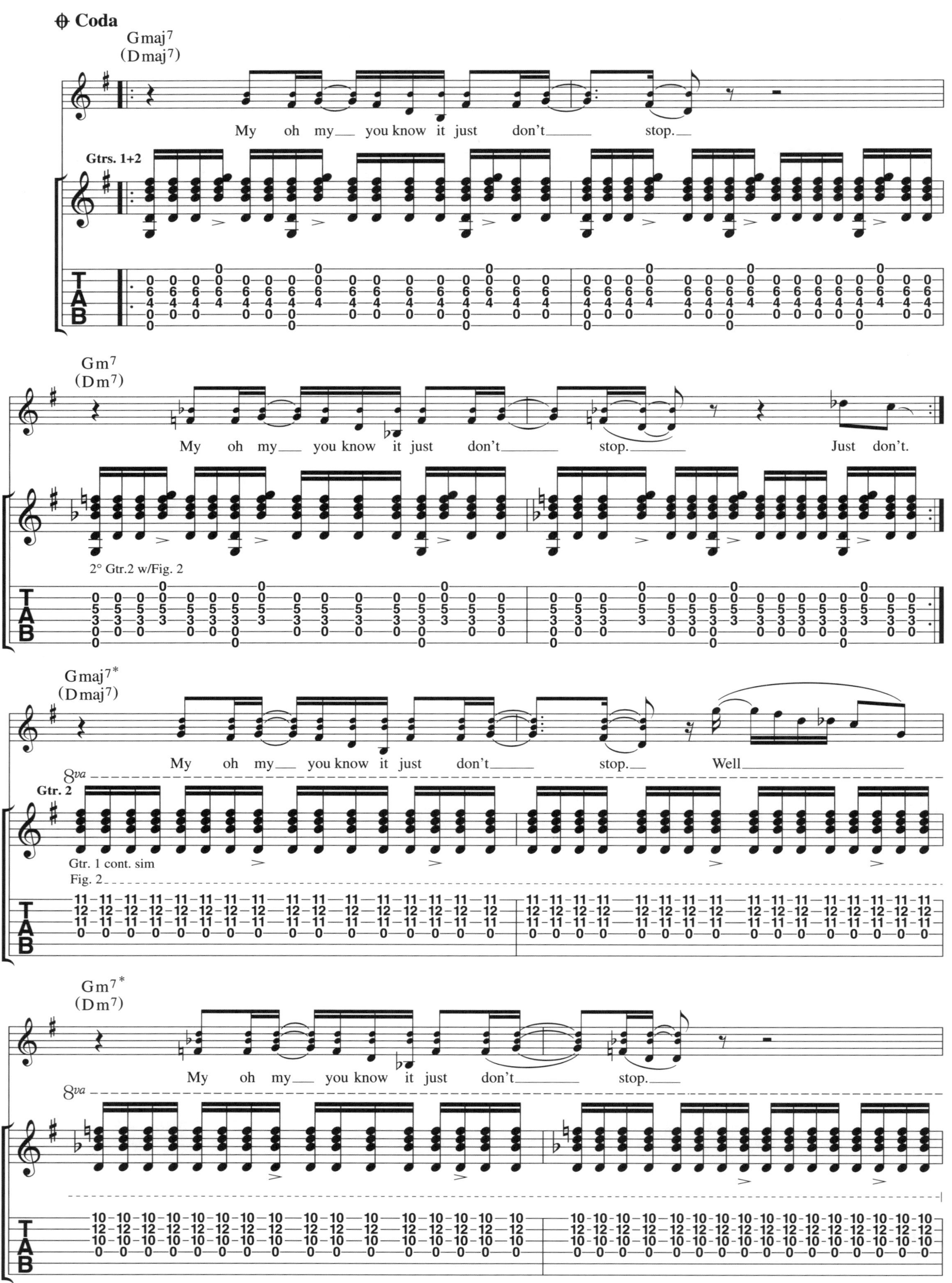
Coda
Gmaj7
(Dmaj7)
My oh my you know it just don't stop.
Gtrs. 1+2
Gm7
(Dm7)
My oh my you know it just don't stop.
Just don't.
2° Gtr.2 w/Fig. 2
Gmaj7*
(Dmaj7)
My oh my you know it just don't stop.
Well
8va
Gtr. 2
Gtr. 1 cont. sim
Fig. 2
Gm7*
(Dm7)
My oh my you know it just don't stop.
8va

Gmaj7*
(Dmaj7)
My oh my___ you know it just don't_____ stop.___
8va

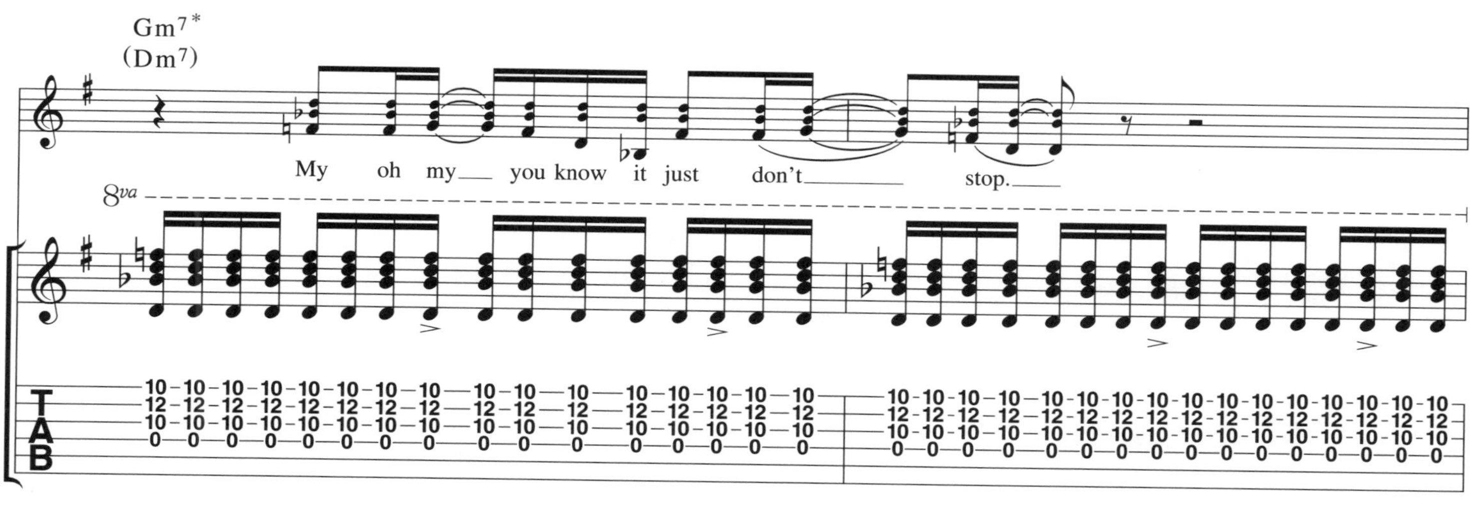
Gm7*
(Dm7)
My oh my___ you know it just don't_____ stop.___
8va

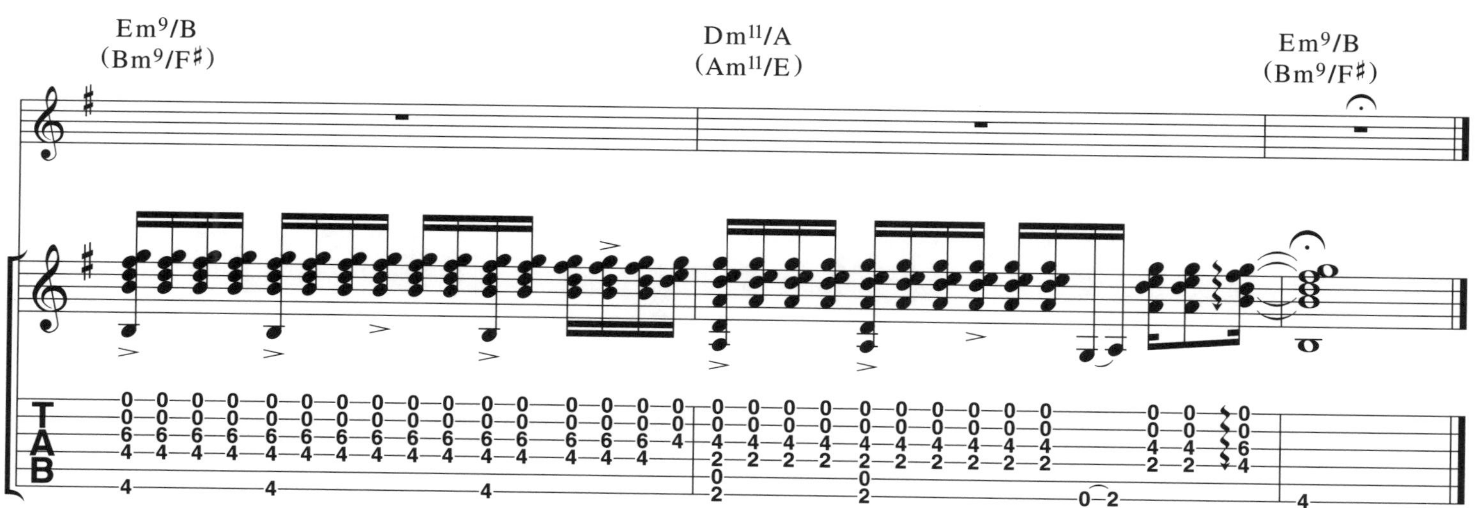
Em9/B
(Bm9/F♯)
Dm11/A
(Am11/E)
Em9/B
(Bm9/F♯)

Nightblindness

Words & Music by David Gray

Bm (Am)
A (G)
— past e - ter - ni - ty, — here — lis -
Gmaj7 (Fmaj7)
D/A (C/G)
- ten - ing — to the si - rens — com - ing clos -
Bm (Am)
F♯m (Em)
- er, now fur - ther a - way. —
Chorus
Em (Dm)
A (G)
Bm (Am)
A (G)
What we gon - na do when the mon - ey runs out?
TAB

Em
(Dm)
A
(G)
Bm
(Am)
A
(G)
I wish that there was some-thing left to say.
Em
(Dm)
A
(G)
F♯
(E)
F♯7
(E7)
Where we gon - na find the eyes to see a bright - er day?
Gtr. 1 cont. in slashes
Gmaj7
(Fmaj7)
D/A
(C/G)
Bm
(Am)
Gtr. 1
cont. sim.
Gtr. 2 (elec.)
mf let ring . . . w/tremelo
A
(G)
Verse
Gmaj7
(Fmaj7)
D/A
(C/G)
2. Sick of all the same old ans - wers, lost chan -

Bm
(Am)
A
(G)
Gmaj7
(Fmaj7)
- ces, cold stones, prop-ping moun - tains up on match -
D/A
(C/G)
Bm
(Am)
A
(G)
- sticks drag-ging bas - kets full of bones. Hon-ey please
Gmaj7
(Fmaj7)
Gtr. 1
D/A
(C/G)
Bm
(Am)
cont. sim.
don't stop your talk - ing, 'cos there's a feel - ing won't leave me a - lone.
F♯m
(Em)
Chorus
Em
(Dm)
A
(G)
Bm
(Am)
A
(G)
What we gon-na do when the mon-ey run out?
TAB

Em
(Dm)
A
(G)
Bm
(Am)
A
(G)
I wish that there was some-thing I could say.
Em
(Dm)
A
(G)
F♯
(E)
F♯7
(E7)
How we gon-na find the eyes to see a bright - er day?
Gmaj7
(Fmaj7)
A
(G)
Bm
(Am)
A
(G)
Gtr. 1
cont. sim.
What we gon-na do when the - mon-ey runs out?
Em
(Dm)
A
(G)
Bm
(Am)
A
(G)
I wish there was some-thing left to say.

Em
(Dm)
A
(G)
F♯
(E)
F♯7
(E7)
How we gon - na find the eyes__ to see____ a bright - er day?__
Gmaj7
(Fmaj7)
D/A
(C/G)
Bm
(Am)
A
(G)
A bright - er day.
Gmaj7
(Fmaj7)
D/A
(C/G)
Bm
(Am)
A
(G)
A bright - er day.
Gmaj7
(Fmaj7)
D/A
(C/G)
Bm
(Am)
A
(G)
Repeat ad lib to fade
A bright - er day.

We're not right

Words & Music by David Gray, Craig McClune & Lestyn Polson

E
B
We can't tell the bot - tle from the moun -
C♯m
A*
To Coda
1.
E
A/D
- tain top; no we're not right.
1. cont.
E
A/D
2.
E
B
We can't tell the bot - tle from the moun - tain top; now my
C♯m

F♯
A*
hands are shak - ing but I just can't stop.
B
C♯m
A*
Can't tell the bot - tle from the moun - tain top; no we're not right.
E
A/D
E
G
A*
F♯
E
A/D
E
TAB

B
C♯m
Can't tell the bot - tle from the moun - tain top; now my knees
F♯
A
are shak - ing, but I just can't stop.
B
C♯m
A*
We can't tell the bot - tle from the moun - tain top; no we're not right.
E
A/D
E
A/D
D.𝄋 al Coda ⊕

Verse 3: Now I'm weak and my head is sore
And I feel like I can't go on no more
Come in here where normal rules do not apply
Can't tell the bottle . . . *etc.*

White ladder

Words & Music by David Gray, Craig McClune & Lestyn Polson

Aadd9
C♯m7
Badd11
for - ev - er cry'n'
how many times
Bm11
Aadd9
C♯m7
oh, time.
oh, Lord?
I don't wan -
I don't wan -
Badd11
Bm11
Aadd9
- na feel to - night.
- na feel no more.
Am9
G6
There's no rhyme or rea - - - - - - - - son to love

F♯7add11
G6
this sweet love.
1.
2,3.
E
Yeah. To the night,
Gtr. 1 w/Fig. 1
Chorus
D
Dsus2
E7
another body, to the night, another name.
mf
3° Gtr. 1 w/Fig. 1
4° tacet
To the night, another valentine, a burn-
TAB

1,3.
2.
D
Dsus2
To Coda
E7
E7
D.S. al Coda
- ing flame. To the night,
Coda
E7
Cadd9
To the night, an - oth - er bo -
Dadd9/11
- dy; to the night, an - oth - er name. To the night,
D
Dsus2
E7
D
an - oth - er va - len - tine, a burn - ing flame.

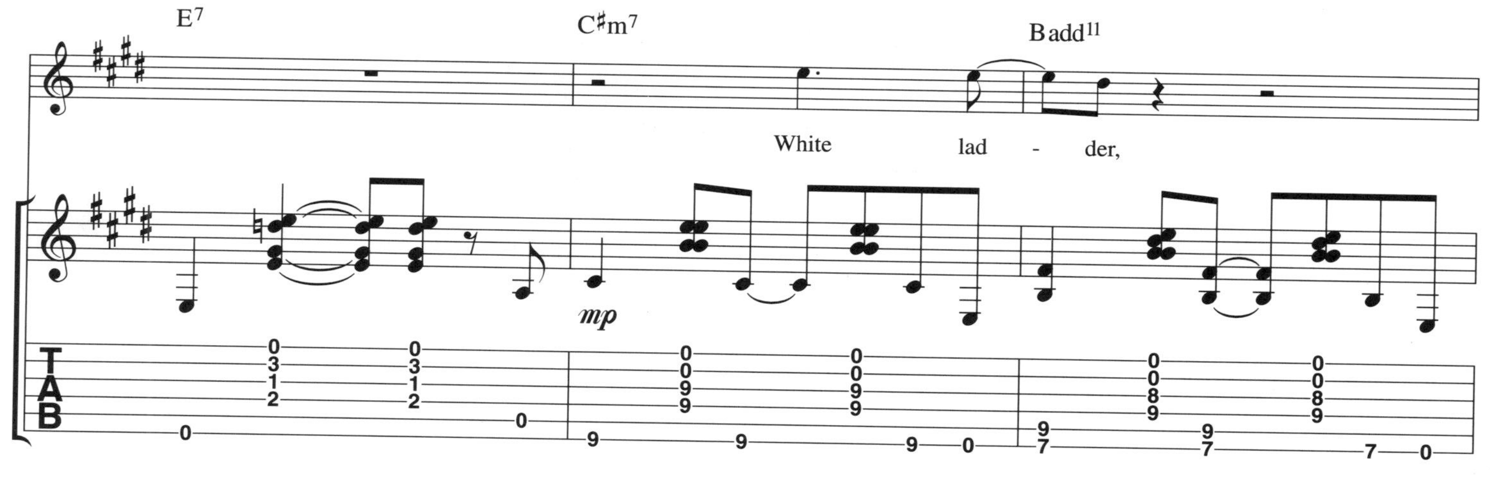

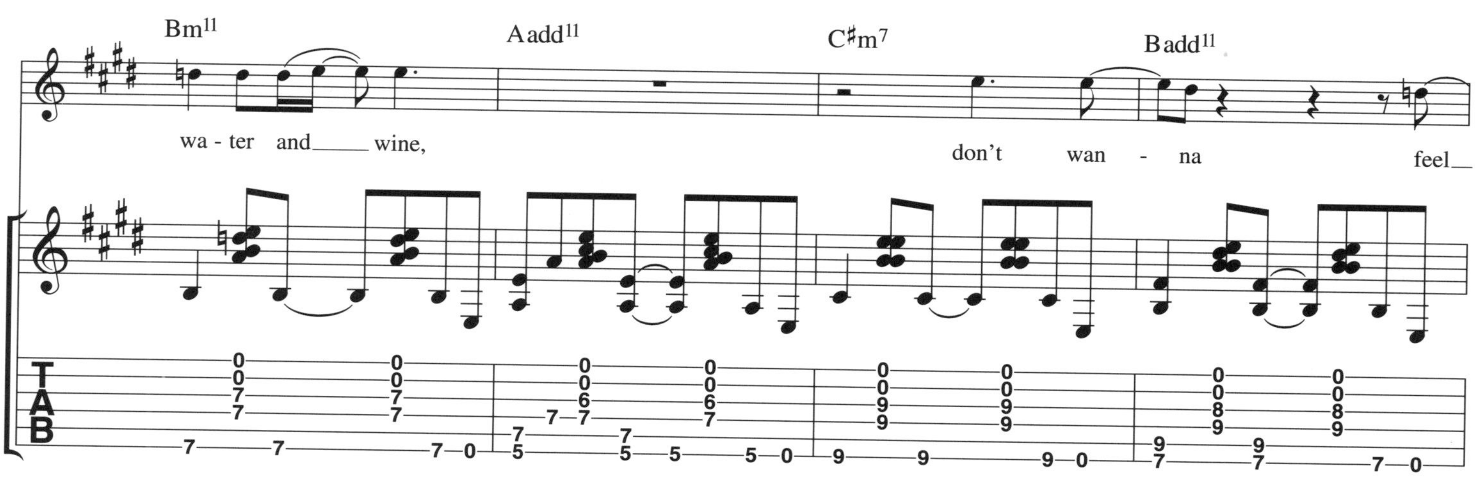

Verse 3:

Tall order, tremble and sigh
Forever crying, oh my, yeah, yeah, yeah
I don't wanna feel tonight
There's no rhyme or reason
To love, this sweet, sweet love.

Silver lining

Words & Music by David Gray

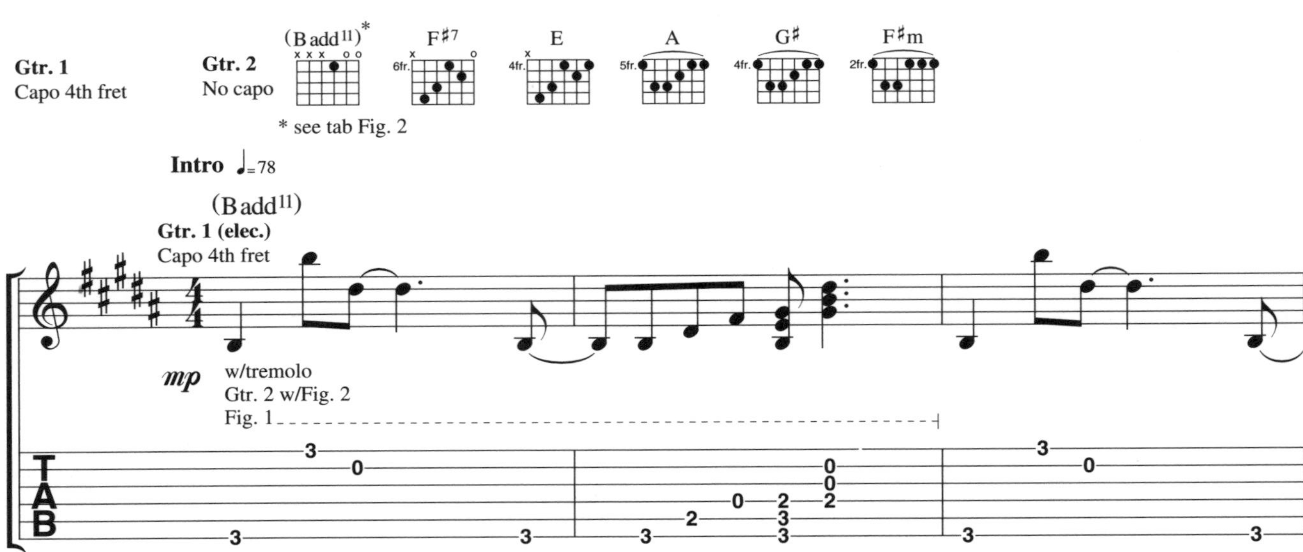

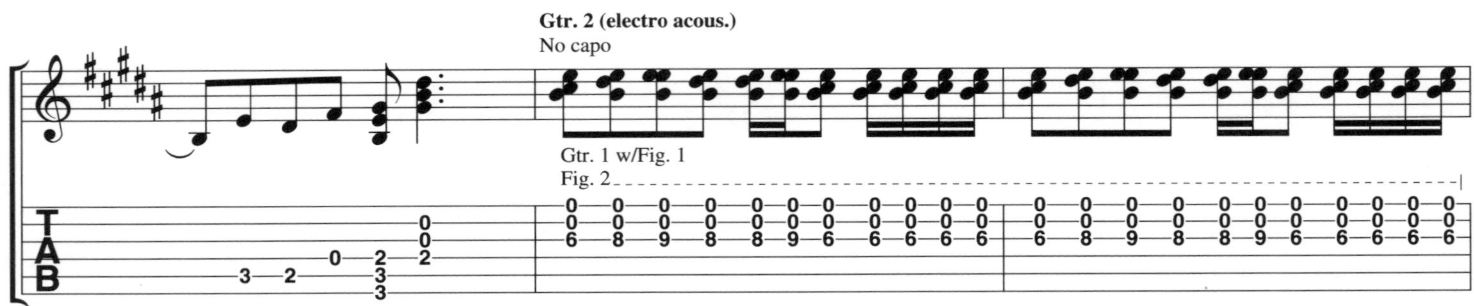

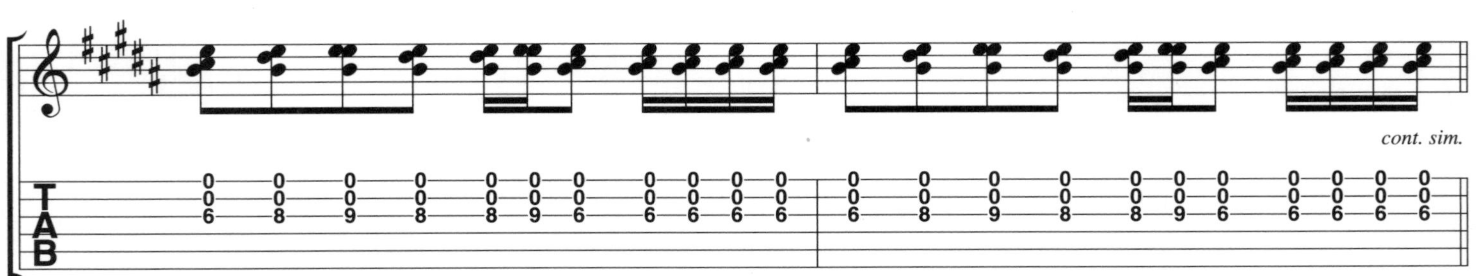

Verse
(Badd11)
(E bass)
(B bass)
1. Take this sil-ver lin - ing keep it in your own sweet head,
2. Step in-to the sil - ence, take it in your own two hands,
Gtr. 1
Gtr. 2 w/Fig. 2 ad lib sim.
(G♯ bass)
(B bass)
(E bass)
and shine it when the night is burn-ing red.
and scat-ter it like dia - monds all a-cross this land.
(B bass)
(G♯ bass)
(B bass)
Yeah,
Shine it in the twi - light, shine it on the cold, cold ground.
Blaze it in the morn - ing, wear it like an iron skin.
(E bass)
(B bass)
(G♯ bass)

(B bass)
(E bass)
(B bass)
Shine it till these walls come tumb-ling down.
On - ly things worth liv-ing for are in-no-cence and ma - - - gic, a - men.
(G♯bass)
Chorus
Gtr. 2
F♯7
E
cont. sim.
We were born with our eyes wide op - en,
mf
F♯7
E
F♯7
so a - live with wild hope. Now can you tell me why,
A
(B add11)
A
time af - ter time, they drag you down, down in the dark - ness
TAB

(Badd11)
A
G♯
deep?
Fools in their mad - ness all a - round
F♯m
E
To Coda
Gtr. 2
know that the light don't sleep.
mp
Instrumental
N.C.
piano
Gtr. 2 tacet
let ring . . .

let ring . . .
D.𝄋 al Coda
cont. sim.
We were
Coda
F♯m
E
know that the light don't sleep.
A
(Badd11)
Time af-ter time they drag you down, down

A
(Badd11)
A
in the dark - ness deep.
Fools
in their mad - ness all
G♯
F♯m
E
a - round
know that the light don't sleep,
F♯m
E
know that the light don't sleep.
Gtr. 2
(Badd11)
mp
Gtr. 2 w/Fig. 2 sim.

This year's love

Words & Music by David Gray

Tune gtr.
⑥ = E ③ = G
⑤ = A ② = B
④ = D ① = D
Capo 1st fret

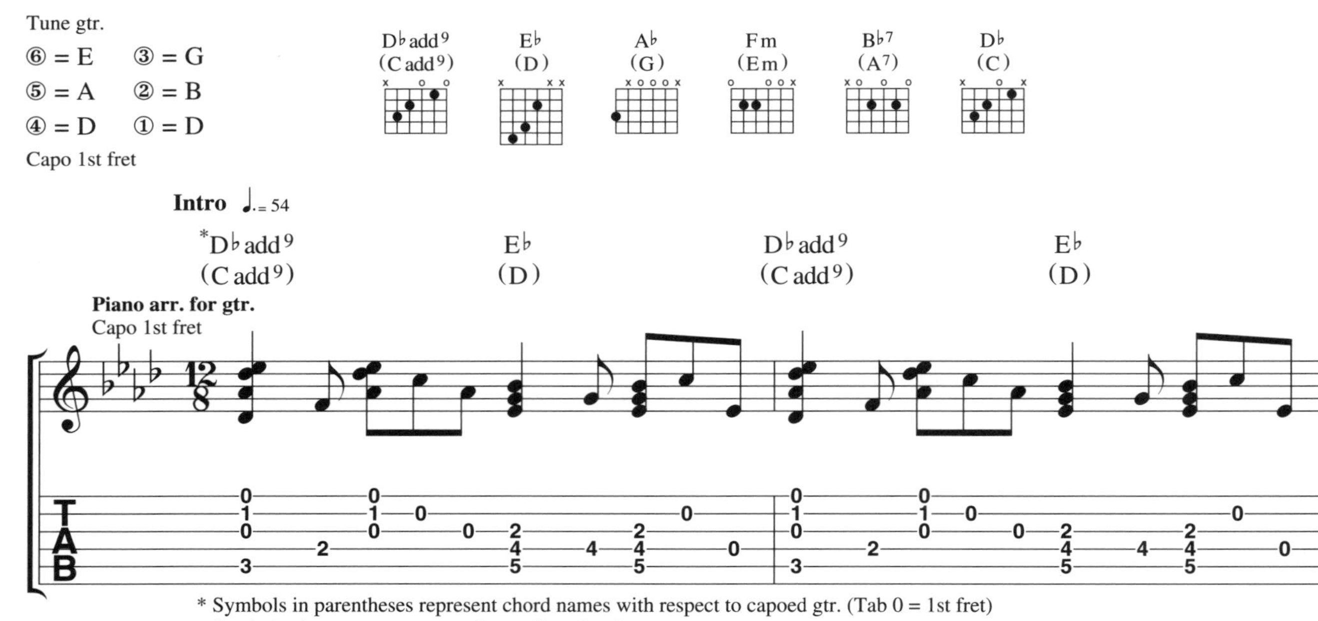

* Symbols in parentheses represent chord names with respect to capoed gtr. (Tab 0 = 1st fret)
Symbols above represent actual sounding chords.

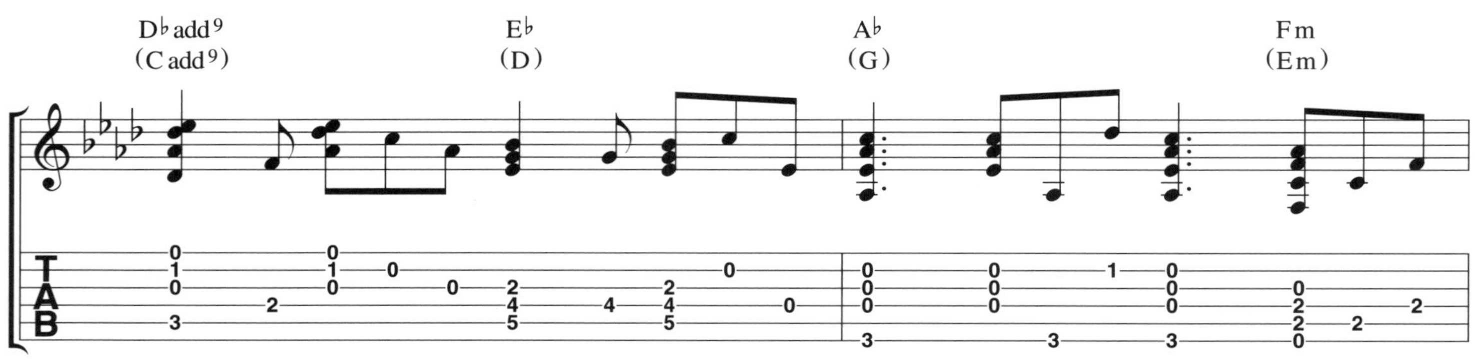

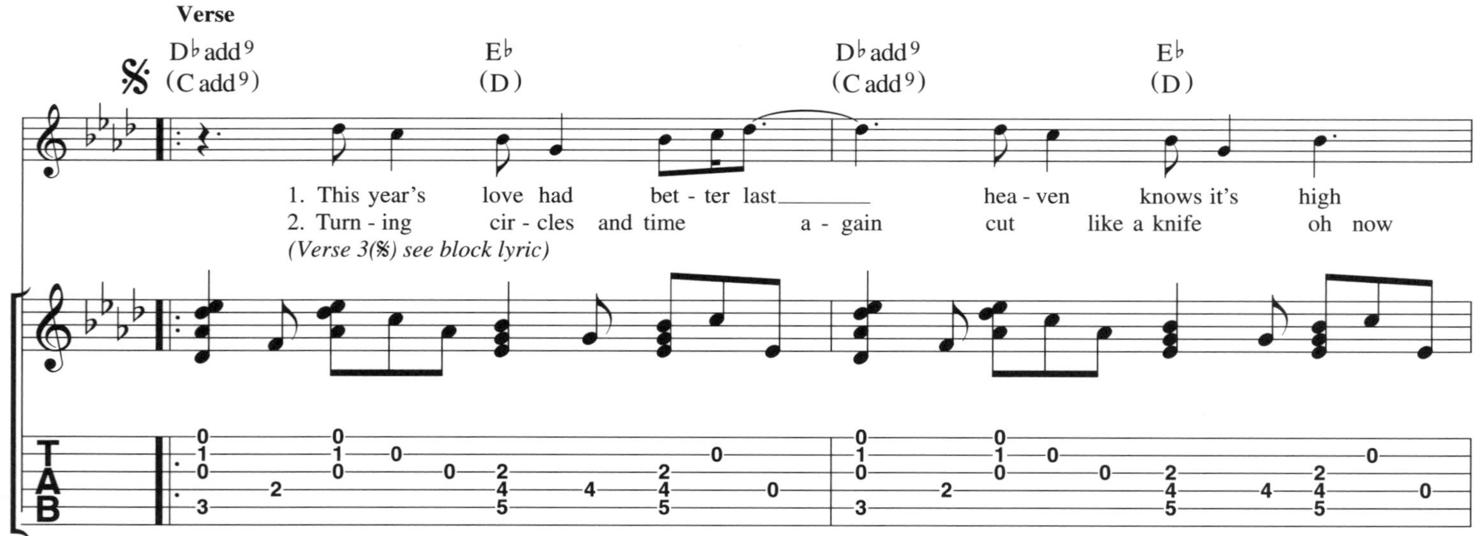

D♭add9 (Cadd9)
E♭ (D)
A♭ (G)
Fm (Em)
time. I've been wait - ing on my own too long.
if you love me got to know for sure.
D♭add9 (Cadd9)
E♭ (D)
D♭add9 (Cadd9)
E♭ (D)
And when you hold me like you do it feels so right, oh now,
Cos it takes some-thing more this time than sweet, sweet lies, oh now,
D♭add9 (Cadd9)
E♭ (D)
A♭ (G)
I start to for - get how my heart gets torn when that
be-fore I op - en up my arms and fall los - ing
Fm (Em)
1.
B♭7 (A7)
D♭ (C)
hurt gets thrown; feel - ing like I can't go on.
all con - trol ev - 'ry
TAB

2.3.
B♭7 (A7)
D♭ (C)
A♭ (G)
dream in - side my soul, when you kiss me on that mid - night street, sweep me
know this life goes on won't you kiss me on that
Fm (Em)
B♭7 (A7)
D♭ (C)
D.S. al Coda
To Coda
off my feet, sing - ing ain't this life so sweet?
Coda
D♭add9 (Cadd9)
E♭ (D)
This year's love had bet - ter last.
This year's love had bet - ter last.

Verse 3:

This year's love had better last
This year's love had better last
'Cause who's to worry if our hearts get torn
When that hurt gets thrown
Don't you know this life goes on?
Won't you kiss me (*etc.*)

Sail away

Words & Music by David Gray

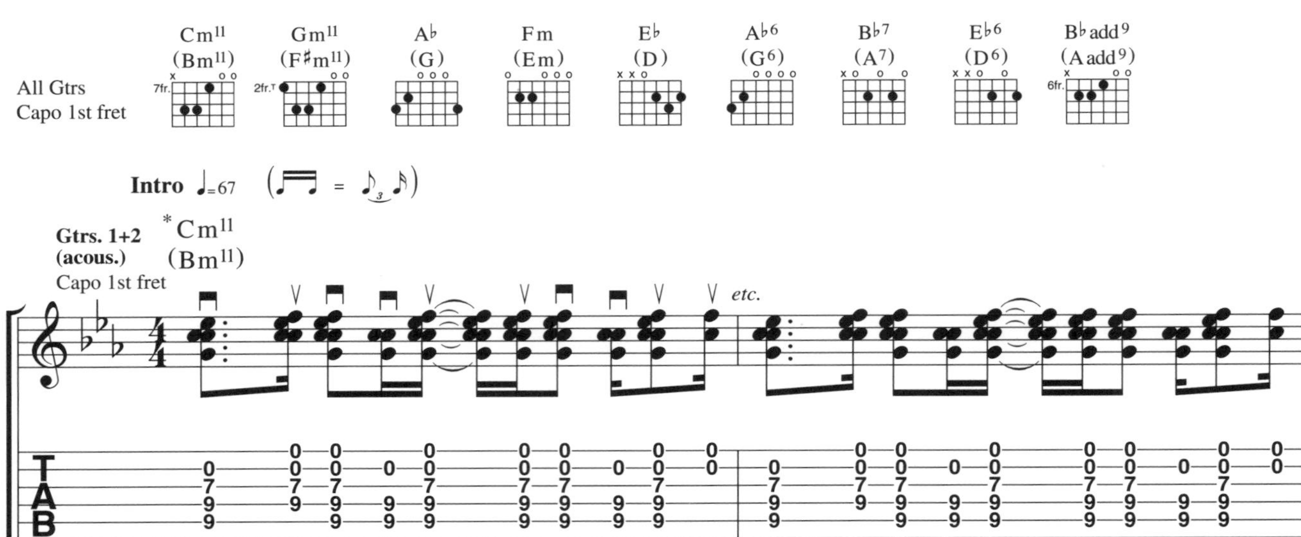

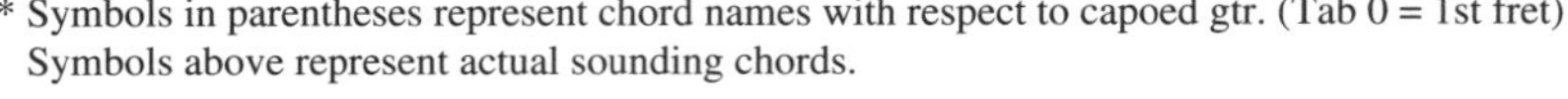
* Symbols in parentheses represent chord names with respect to capoed gtr. (Tab 0 = 1st fret)
Symbols above represent actual sounding chords.

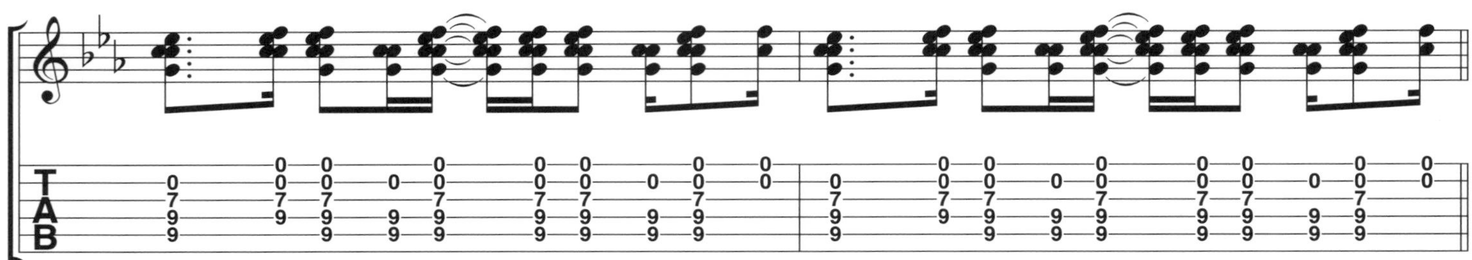

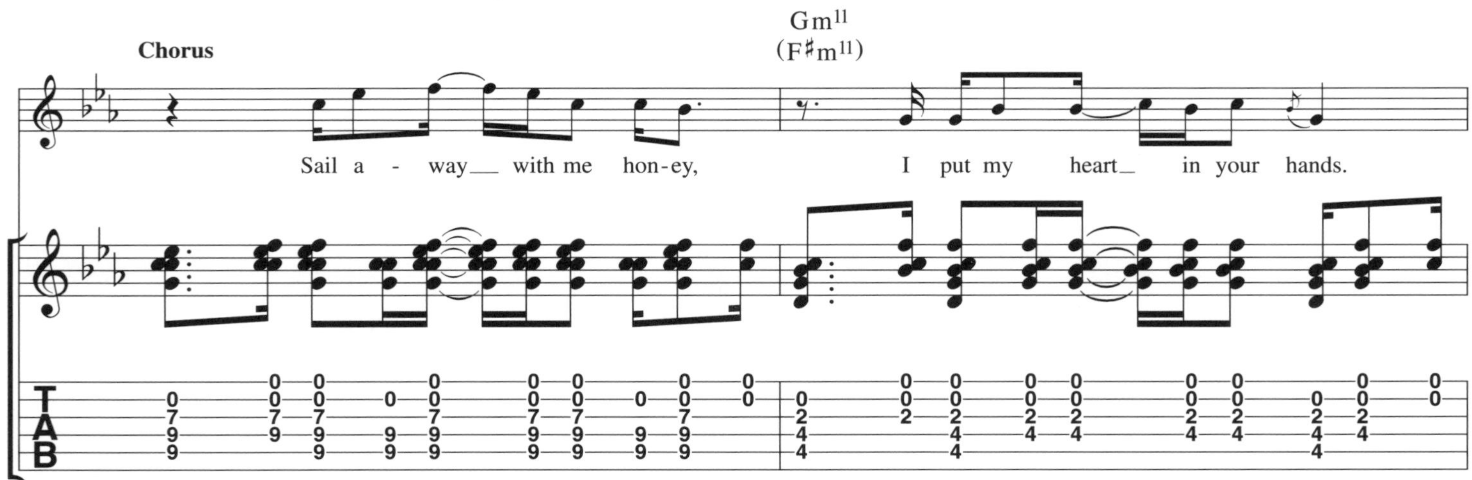

Cm11
(Bm11)
A♭
(G)
Fm
(Em)
Sail a - way with me hon - ey now, now, now.
Cm11
(Bm11)
E♭
(D)
A♭
(G)
Fm
(Em)
Sail a - way with me; what will be will be.
A♭6
(G6)
B♭7
(A7)
Fm
(Em)
I wan - na hold you now, now, now.
Verse
E♭6
(D6)
Gm11
(F♯m11)
1. Cra - zy skies all wild a - bove me now,
etc.

E♭6
(D6)
Gm11
(F♯m11)
win-ter howl - ing at my face;
E♭6
(D6)
Gm11
(F♯m11)
and ev - 'ry - thing I held so dear
Cm11
(Bm11)
B♭add9
(Aadd9)
dis - ap - peared with - out a trace.
Verse
E♭6
(D6)
Gm11
(F♯m11)
2. Though all the times I tast - ed love,
3. I've been talk - ing drunk - en gib - ber - ish,

E♭6
(D6)
Gm11
(F♯m11)
nev - er knew quite what I had.
fall - ing in and out of bars.
E♭6
(D6)
Gm11
(F♯m11)
Lit - tle dar - ling if you hear me now,
Trying to get some ex - plan - a - tion here,
Cm11
(Bm11)
B♭add9
(Aadd9)
nev - er need - ed you so bad;
for the way some peo - ple are;
A♭
(G)
Fm
(Em)
2. only
spin - ning 'round - in - side my head.
how did it ever come so far?

Chorus
Cm11
(Bm11)
Gm11
(F♯m11)
Sail a - way with me hon-ey, I put my heart in your hands.
Cm11
(Bm11)
A♭
(G)
Fm
(Em)
Sail a - way with me hon-ey now, now, now.
Cm11
(Bm11)
E♭
(D)
A♭
(G)
Fm
(Em)
Sail a - way with me; what will be will be.
A♭6
(G6)
B♭7
(A7)
Fm
(Em)
I wan-na hold you now, now, now.
TAB

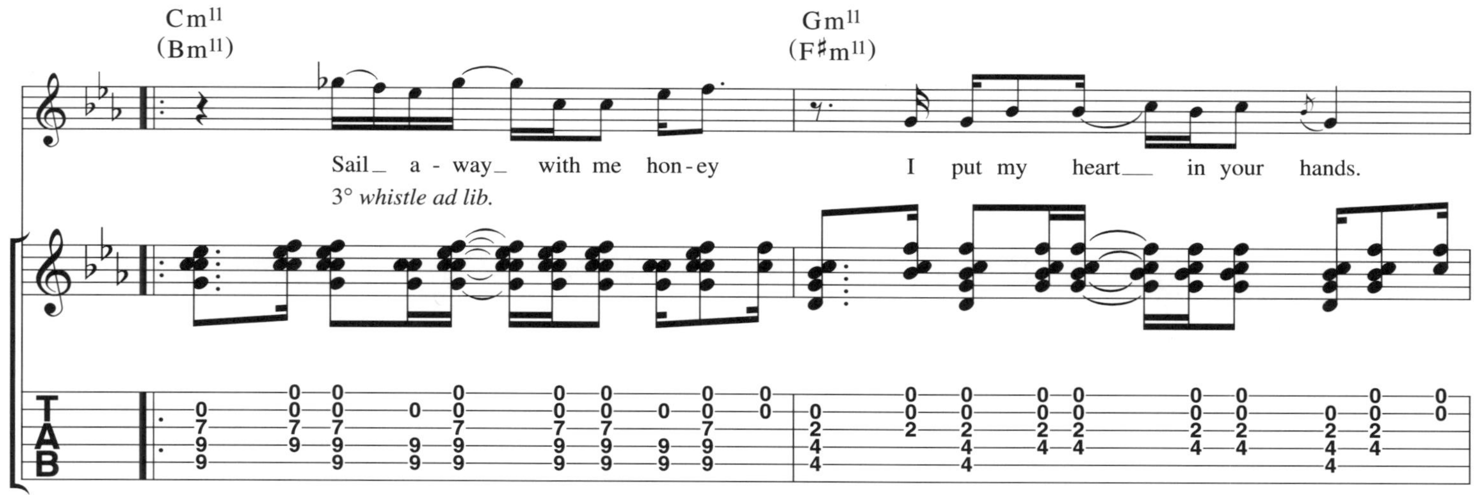
Cm11
(Bm11)
Gm11
(F♯m11)
Sail_ a - way_ with me hon-ey
I put my heart_ in your hands.
3° whistle ad lib.

Cm11
(Bm11)
A♭
(G)
Fm
(Em)
Sail a - way with me hon - ey now,_ now,
2. It break me up if you pull me down,_ woh

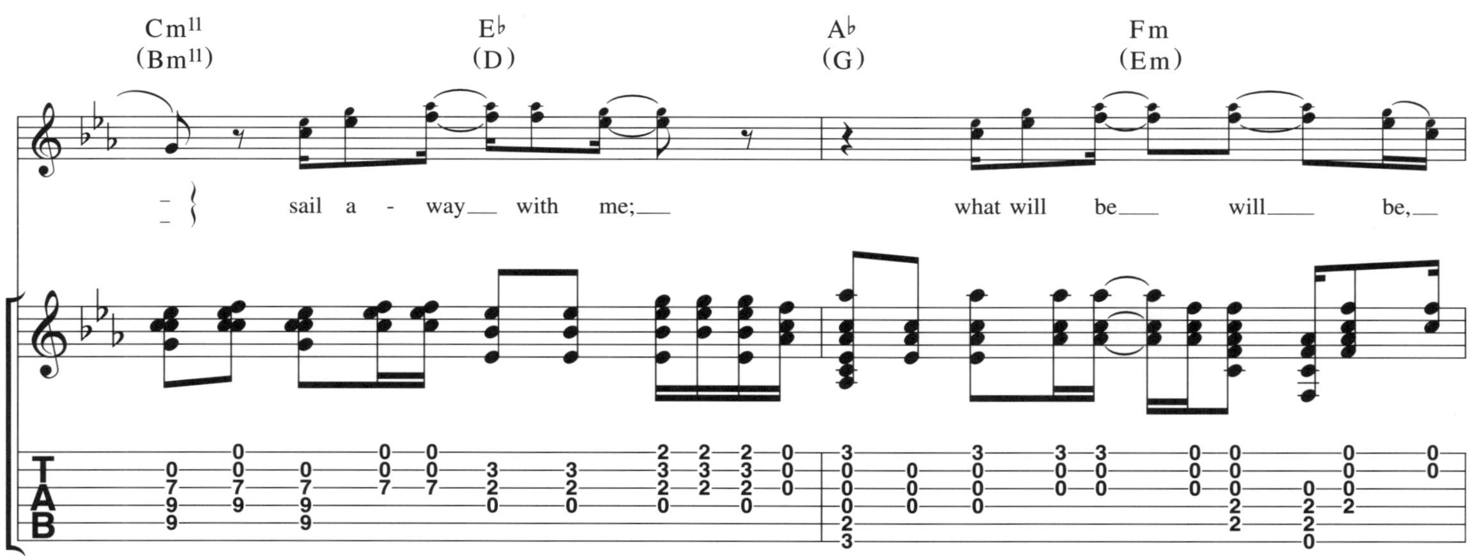
Cm11
(Bm11)
E♭
(D)
A♭
(G)
Fm
(Em)
sail a - way_ with me;_
what will be_ will_ be,_

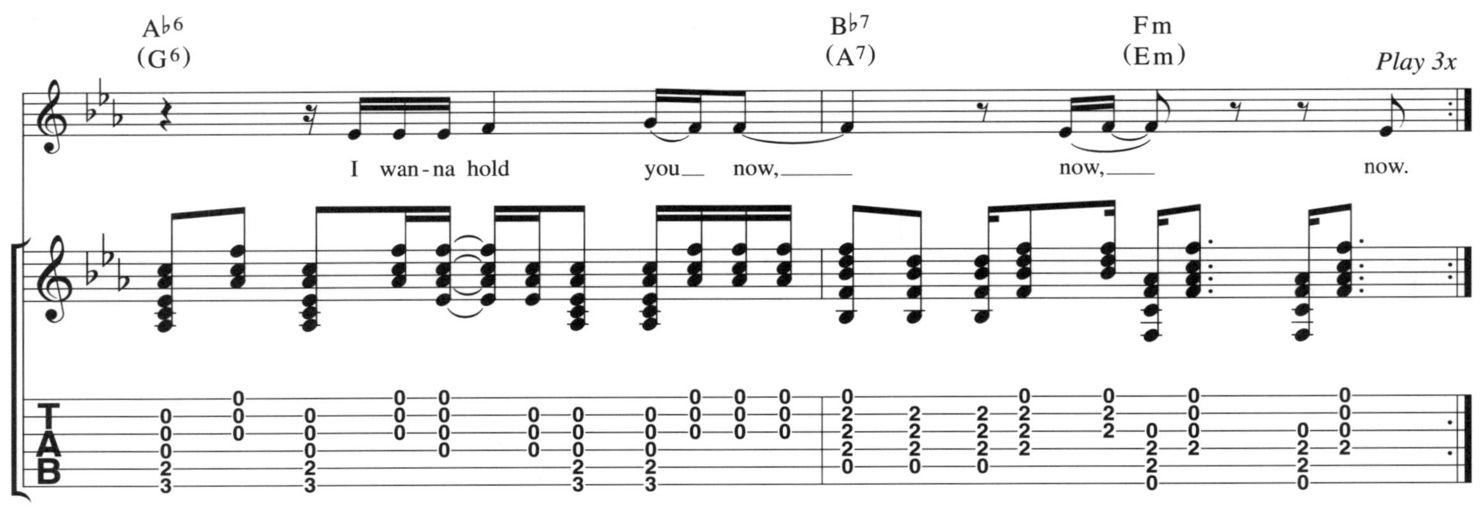

A♭6
(G6)
B♭7
(A7)
Fm
(Em)
Play 3x
I wan-na hold you now, now, now.

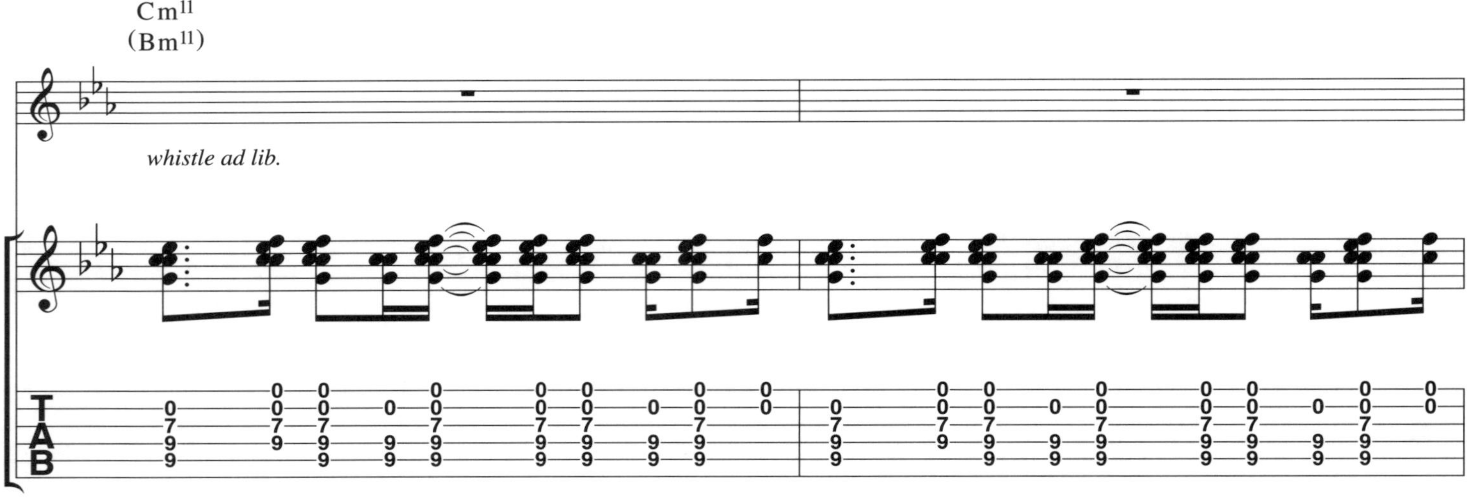

Cm11
(Bm11)
whistle ad lib.

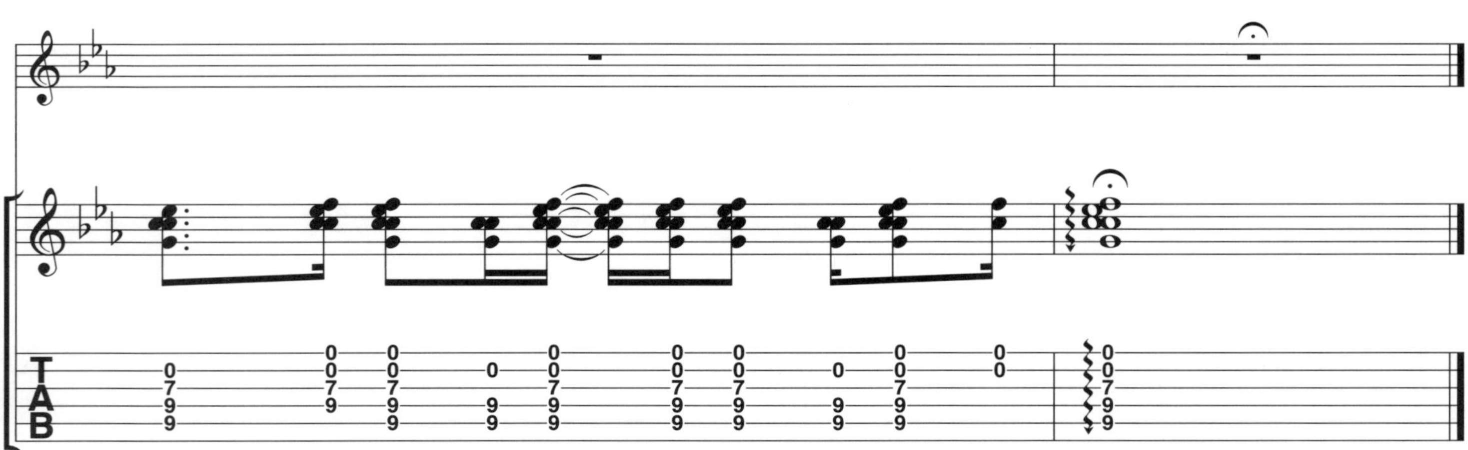

Say hello wave goodbye

Words & Music by Marc Almond & David Ball

A
(G)
Dmaj7
(Cmaj7)
E add 6/11
(D add 6/11)
in the rain.
in a suit, but it just wasn't me.
Here was a kind of so so love, and I'm
You're used to wear - ing less and now your life's a mess
gon - na make sure it doesn't hap - pen a - gain.
so in - se - cure you see.
You and I had to be the
I put up with all the scenes, and this is one scene that's
TAB

A
(G)
Dmaj7
(Cmaj7)
Eadd6/11
(Dadd6/11)
standing joke of the year.
going to be played my way.
Omit 2°
You were a run-around, a lost and found,
Omit 2° cont.
and not for me I feel.
Chorus
Dmaj7/F♯
(Cmaj7/E)
Take your hands off me
* harmony 2° & 3°(𝄋) only

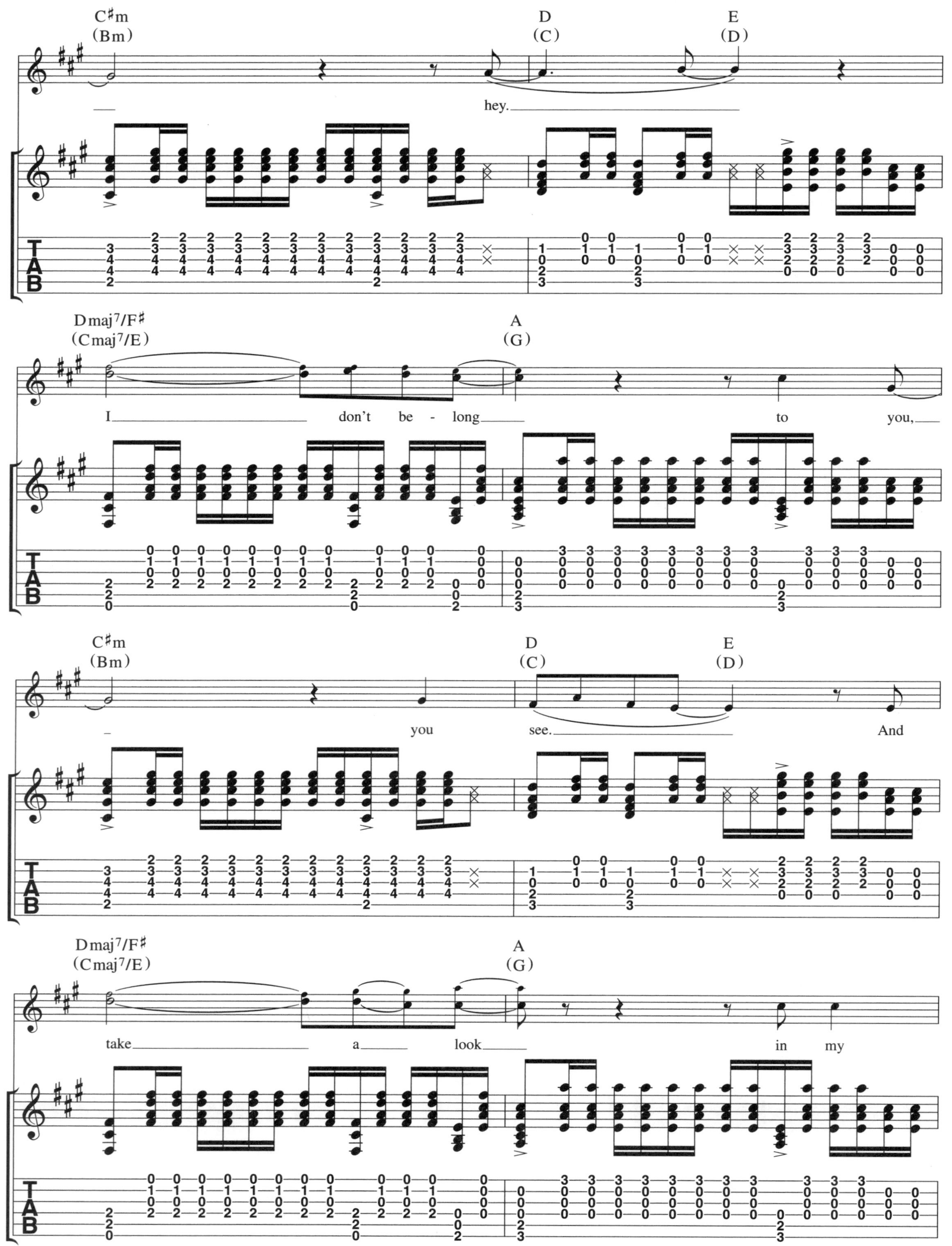
C♯m
(Bm)
D
(C)
E
(D)
hey.
Dmaj7/F♯
(Cmaj7/E)
A
(G)
I don't be - long to you,
C♯m
(Bm)
D
(C)
E
(D)
you see. And
Dmaj7/F♯
(Cmaj7/E)
A
(G)
take a look in my

C♯m
(Bm)
face
for the last
D
(C)
time.
E
(D)
F♯m
(Em)
I nev - er knew you,
A
(G)
you nev - er knew me,
C♯m
(Bm)
say hel - lo good - - - bye.
D
(C)
E
(D)
To Coda
A
(G)
Say hel - lo
Dmaj7
(Cmaj7)
and wave good - - - bye.
E add 6/11
(D add 6/11)
2° Gtr. 2 w/Fig. 1
TAB

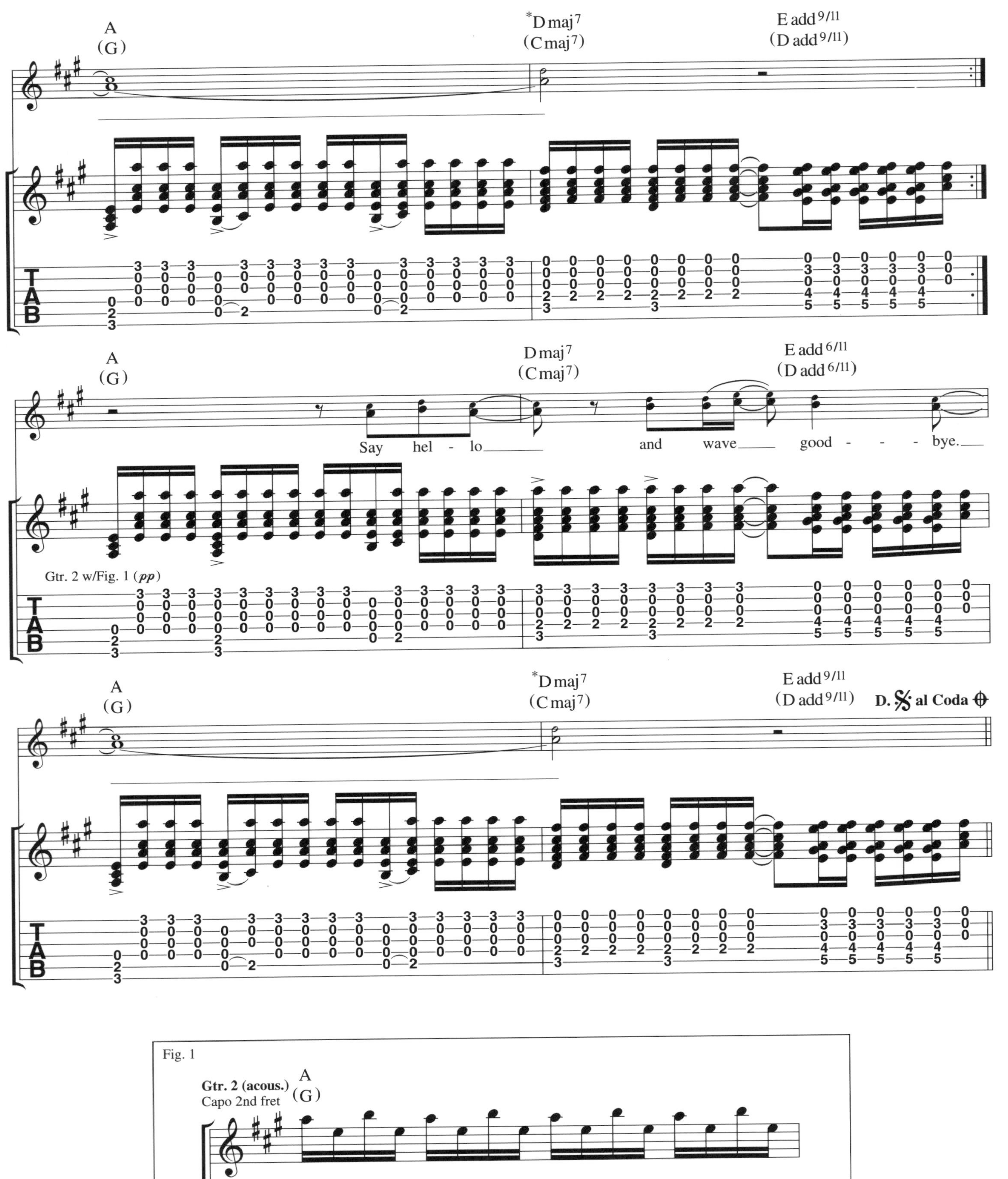
A
(G)
*D maj7
(C maj7)
E add 9/11
(D add 9/11)
A
(G)
D maj7
(C maj7)
E add 6/11
(D add 6/11)
Say hel - lo and wave good - - - bye.
Gtr. 2 w/Fig. 1 (pp)
A
(G)
*D maj7
(C maj7)
E add 9/11
(D add 9/11)
D.S. al Coda
Fig. 1
Gtr. 2 (acous.)
Capo 2nd fret
A
(G)

Coda

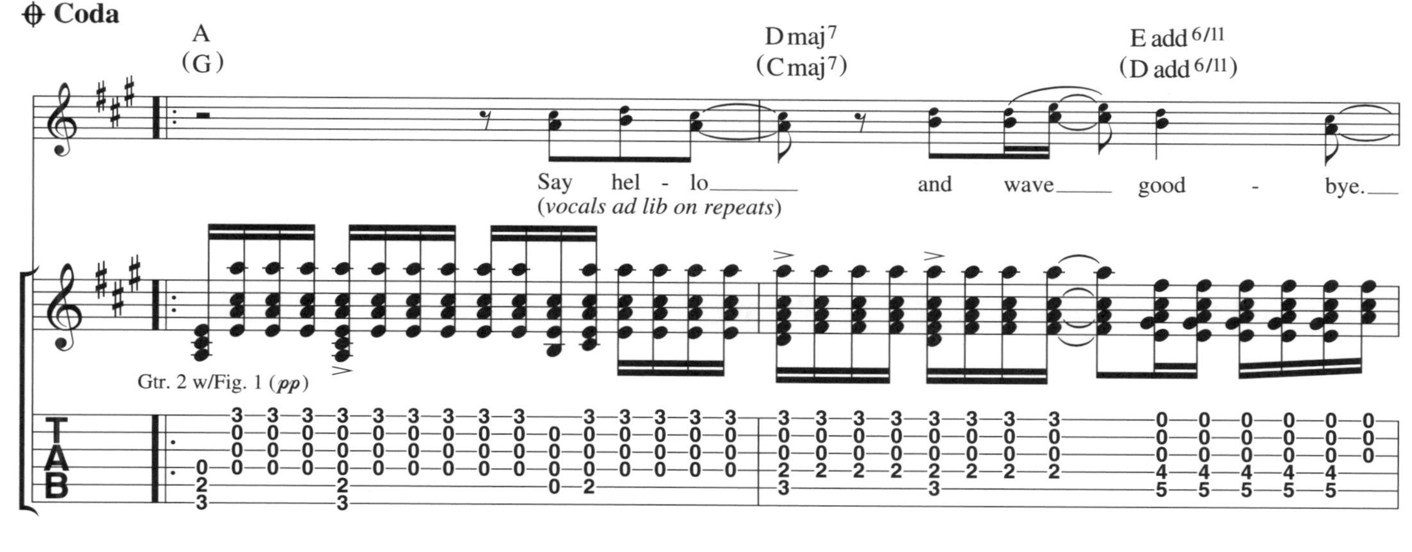
A
(G)
Dmaj7
(Cmaj7)
Eadd6/11
(Dadd6/11)
Say hel - lo and wave good - bye.
(vocals ad lib on repeats)
Gtr. 2 w/Fig. 1 (pp)

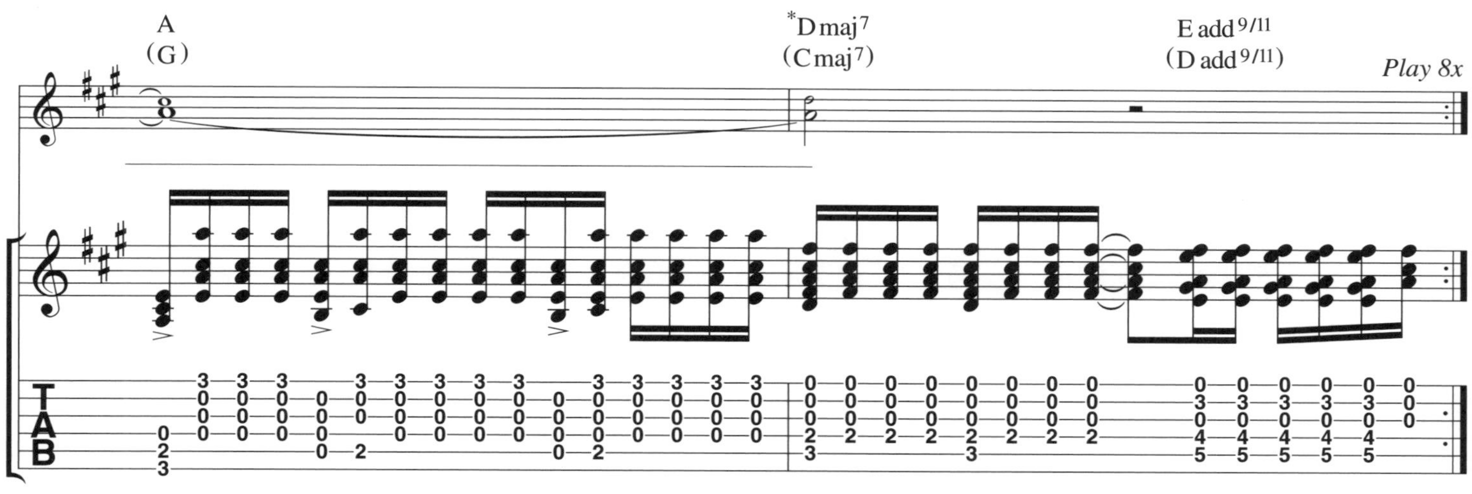
A
(G)
*Dmaj7
(Cmaj7)
Eadd9/11
(Dadd9/11)
Play 8x

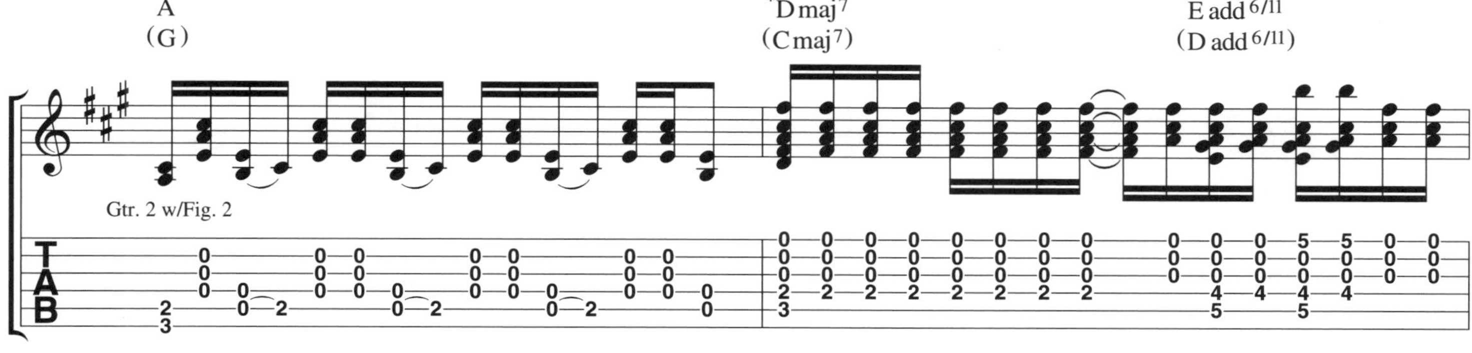
A
(G)
*Dmaj7
(Cmaj7)
Eadd6/11
(Dadd6/11)
Gtr. 2 w/Fig. 2

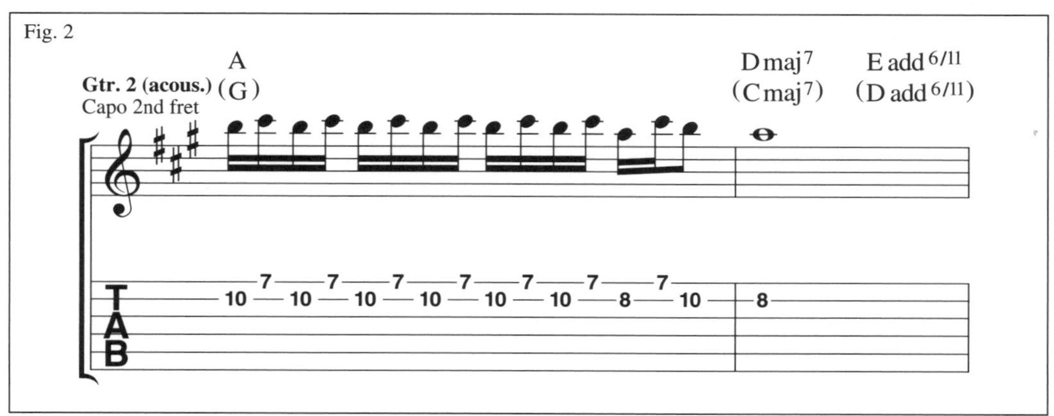
Fig. 2
Gtr. 2 (acous.)
Capo 2nd fret
A
(G)
Dmaj7
(Cmaj7)
Eadd6/11
(Dadd6/11)

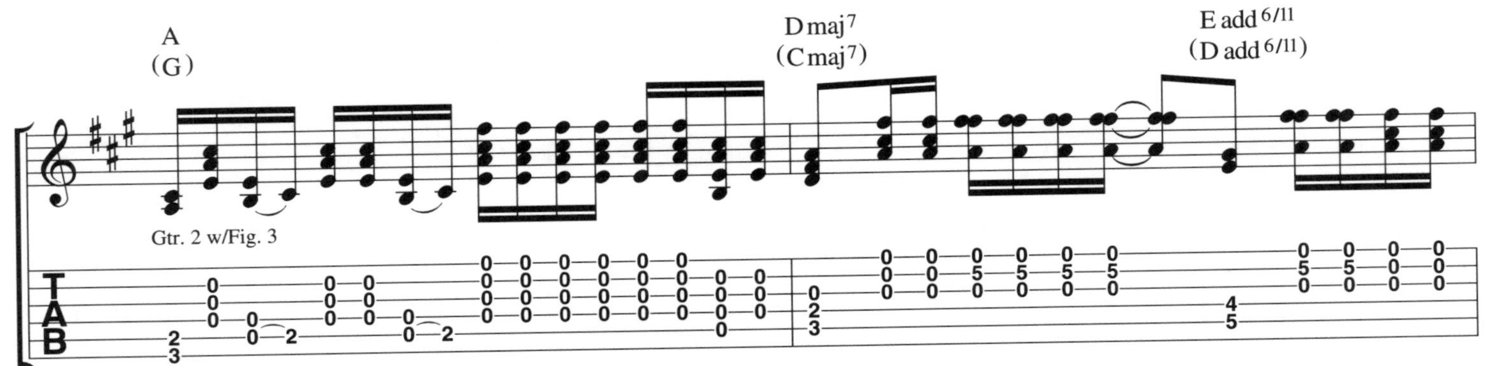
A
(G)
Dmaj7
(Cmaj7)
E add 6/11
(D add 6/11)
Gtr. 2 w/Fig. 3

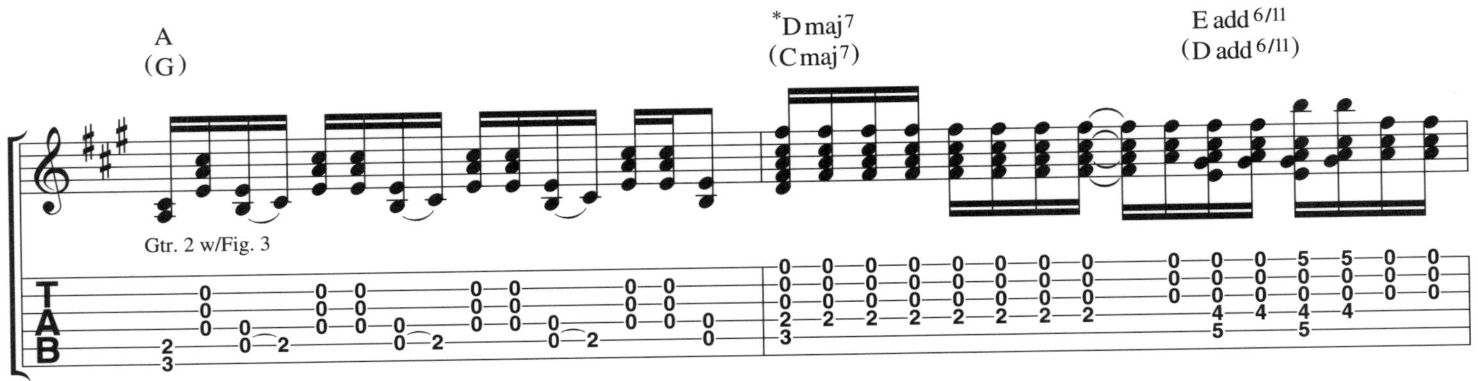
A
(G)
*Dmaj7
(Cmaj7)
E add 6/11
(D add 6/11)
Gtr. 2 w/Fig. 3

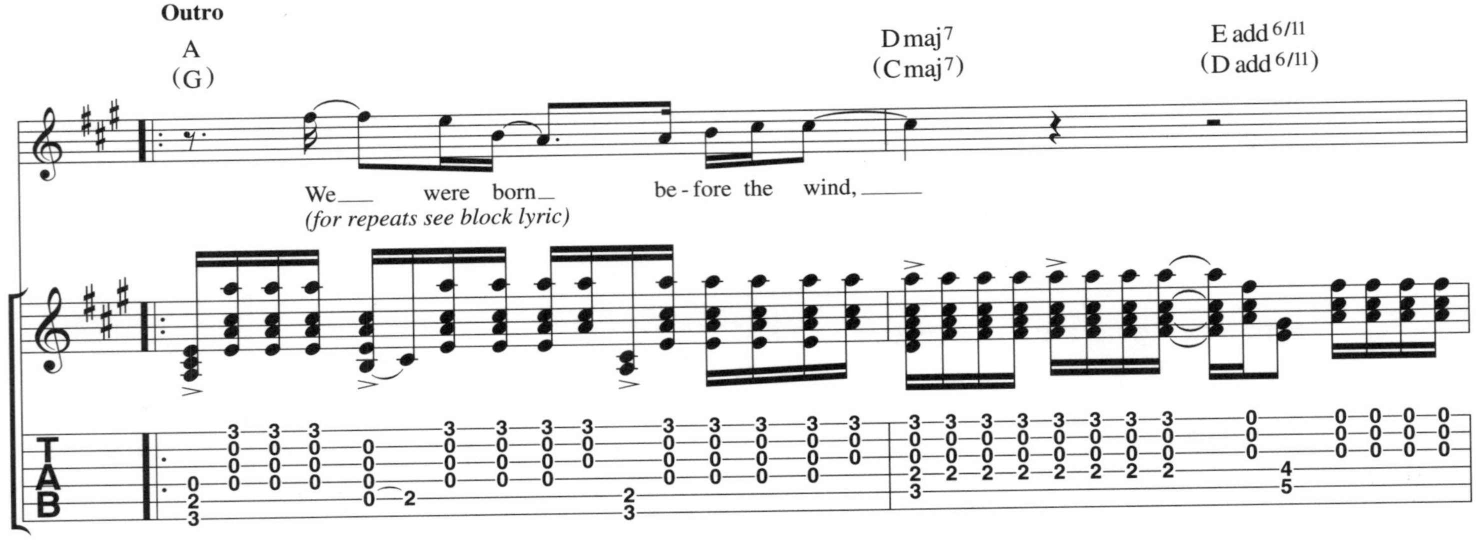
Outro
A
(G)
Dmaj7
(Cmaj7)
E add 6/11
(D add 6/11)
We were born before the wind,
(for repeats see block lyric)

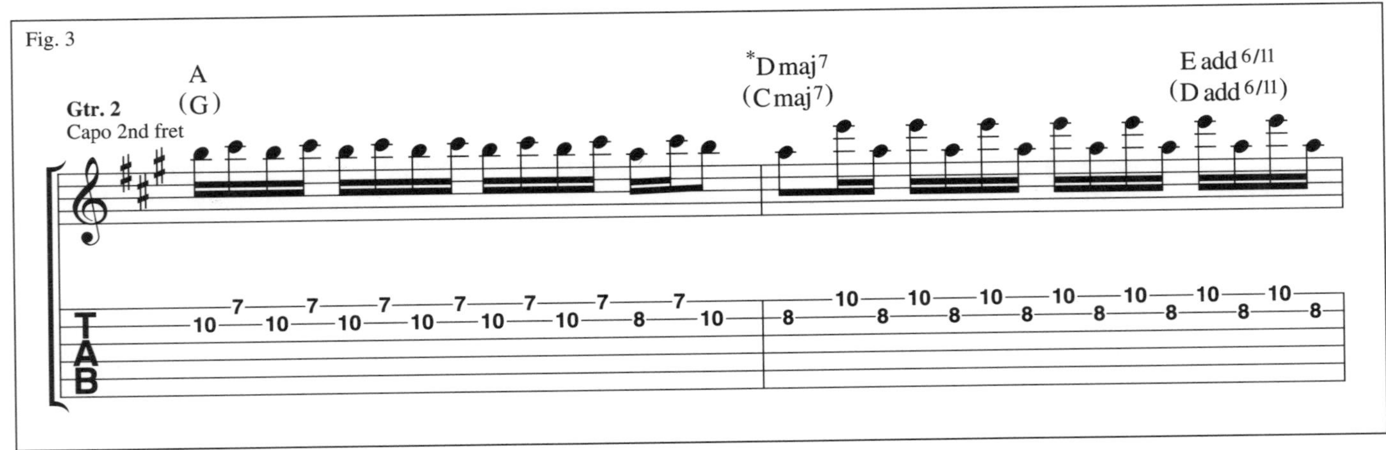
Fig. 3
Gtr. 2
Capo 2nd fret
A
(G)
*Dmaj7
(Cmaj7)
E add 6/11
(D add 6/11)

Verse 3:

Under the deep red light
I can see the make-up sliding down
Well, hey, little girl, you will always make up
So take off that unbecoming frown
As for me, well I'll find someone
Who's not going cheap in the sales
A nice little housewife, who'll give me a steady life
And not keep going off the rails.

**Outro*:

We were born before the wind
Say goodbye
Through the rain, hail, sleet and snow
Say goodbye
Get on the train, the train, the train
Say goodbye
Say goodbye
Say goodbye
Say goodbye
In the wind and the rain my darling,
Say goodbye
In the wind and the rain my darling.

Through to myself

Words & Music by David Gray

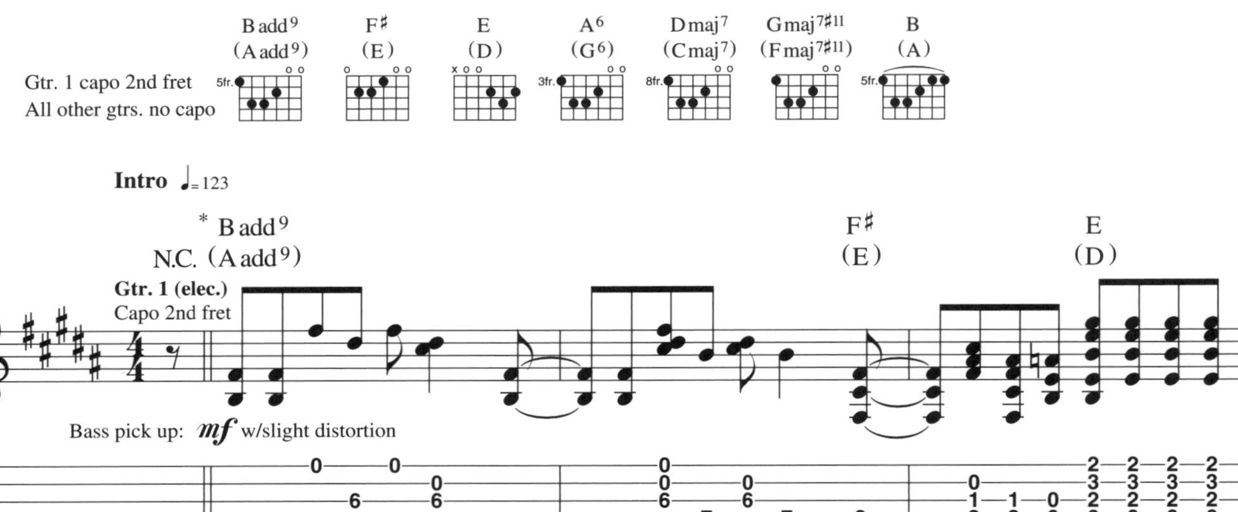

* Symbols in parentheses represent chord names with respect to capoed gtr. (Tab 0 = 2nd fret)
Symbols above represent actual sounding chords.

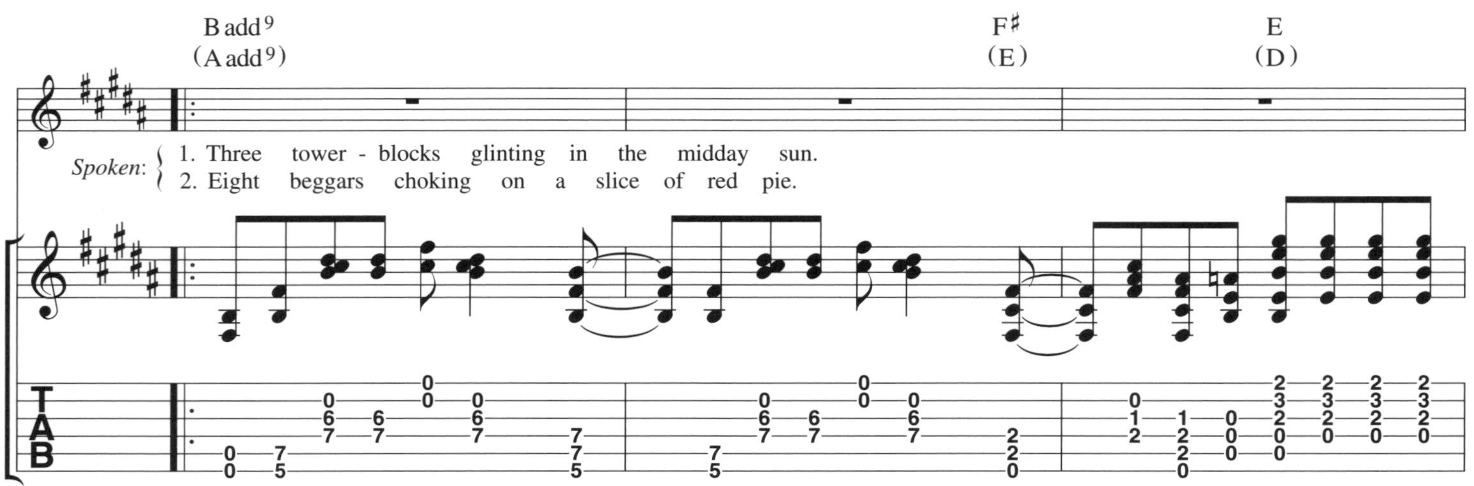

B add9
(A add9)
F♯
(E)
E
(D)
Two ice-cubes melting in a glass of white rum.
Two rivers freezing in a broken goodbye.
Head full of pla - ces where I've___ nev - er gone.___
No hes - i - ta - tion just a___ kick in the eye.___
I can't get through to my - self.___
1.
Just can't get through to my - self.
2.
Just can't get through to my - self.___
A6
(G6)
TAB

Dmaj7 (Cmaj7)
A6 (G6)
Gmaj7♯11 (Fmaj7♯11)
Now we do a lot of learn - ing
Gtr. 2 w/Fig. 1
A6 (G6)
Gmaj7♯11 (Fmaj7♯11)
Dmaj7 (Cmaj7)
A6 (G6)
ev - 'ry day or so it seems. But the road
Gmaj7♯11 (Fmaj7♯11)
F♯ (E)
it keeps re - turn - ing, and I'm right back here a - gain.
Fig. 1
Gtr. 2 (elec.)
No capo
w/clean tone

B add9
(A add9)
F♯
(E)
E
(D)
Spoken: Blue leather jacket and a helium voice.
I can't get through to my - self.
Gtr. 2 w/Fig. 2
Spoken: My head is reeling from too much choice.
I can't get through to my - self.
A6
(G6)
Gtr. 1
Gtr. 3 (elec.)
No capo
Gtr. 1 cont. in slashes
end Fig. 2
w/slight distortion
Fig. 2
Gtr. 2 (elec.)
No capo

E
(D)
B add9
(A add9)
cont. sim.
A6
(G6)
Gmaj7♯11
(Fmaj7♯11)
Just can't get through to my - self.
I can't get through to my - self.
Pre
Full
B
Just can't get through to my - self.
I can't get through to my - self.
I can't get through to my - self.
B
(A)
Gtr. 1
½
¼